HOW COOL WAS
BRIAN HINDLE!

Steve Bradshaw

Published by New Generation Publishing in 2022

Copyright © Steve Bradshaw 2022

First Edition

ISBN   978-1-80369-242-5

www.newgeneration-publishing.com

New Generation Publishing

1 – PROLOGUE... LIFE WITH BRIAN

Hopefully the following pages will help to explain the title of this book and answer that question from my perspective as to, just what an influence Brian Hindle had, not just back then in those 'halcyon' Performing Arts days but, still all these years later, in the life I lead now!

This is an account of my time at The Performing Arts College firstly, as a student then, as a staff member. Without Brian and the other influential staff, my life would have been much the poorer.

Memory does sometimes play funny tricks (as I did whilst at college) but, as far as I can recollect this is how I recall those 'far off memorable times'

My Performing Arts college days, although I didn't realise it at the time, were some of the happiest of my life.

Just everything about those long-gone times, from the unique building, the staff, curriculum and most certainly the students, made it sheer joy to be there and be a part of it for many years.

Performing arts is a wide and varied industry which, for many of us, the course in St Anne's, was our starting point.

Through the doors of The Clifton Drive Campus of Blackpool and The Fylde College, St Anne's, have walked thousands of 'wanna-be' performers, some of which went on to achieve their life ambition, to actually work in the business we call show and perform at the highest level including, stage, screen and TV, whilst others, including myself have gained valuable life skills, which, to this day, have helped me fulfil my life goals.

Brian used to remark in his retirement years that "There wasn't an evening went by when I didn't spot a former student on TV", that was just the tip of the iceberg. He had given that first step up to many students who, had an extremely difficult high ladder to climb!

Listed below are just some of the names who started their journey with Brian. The list is by no means a definitive one, as many more have worked and achieved at the very highest level.

These include:

The Hollywood film director, Peter Chelsom, who, some thirty years later when he came back 'home' to Blackpool to film at the Tower asked to meet Brian. A reunion that brought a tear to Brian's eye, he was overjoyed that Peter had remembered him!

Others include:

David Thewlis
Joanna Riding
Jonnie Moran
Peter Evans
Josie Walker
Vicky Entwistle
Steve Flynn
Jamie Buller
Sean McKenzie
John Simm
Craig Kelly
Dean Kelly
Ken Christian
David Royle
Nicola Palmer
Craig Parkinson
Kate Ford
Ben Heathcote
James Nairn
Jodie Prenger

Their credits are much too long to list and I omitted so many well-known names. Suffice to say Brian was very proud of ALL former students' achievements!

In what turned out to be a prophetic occasion, I decided to grasp the nettle and interview Brian Hindle about his life and times early March 2020, just before the first lockdown.

Little did I know then, this would be the last opportunity to talk to Brian about a 'life well lived', most of which was dedicated to his beloved performing arts, especially encouraging others to achieve their potential!

Brian sadly died later in July 2020. I dedicate this book to Brian and all his wonderful achievements. Thank you!

Where to begin, well the beginning I suppose is a very good place to start!

Brian started the Foundation Drama Course in 1969. From then up until his retirement in 2001, he made a difference to most of the people who crossed that threshold, not just their acting ability, but in life skills such as verbal communication!

Brian obviously didn't do this alone. He brought into the college the backbone of its strength, the staff!

Jim Thomas was a specialist in music and likewise Debbie Smyth in dance, and along with the two Angelas (Moran and Hudson) in Drama, these were to prove the making of my 'halcyon' days at college

The course was that successful that in 1990 Alan Evans, another great stalwart of the college was recruited to head it up, by what now was, an ever-expanding department, from foundation to university level, incorporating all genres of performance.

Brian, I suppose, although I don't know for sure, could have taken on the mantle and title of 'Head of School for Performing Arts' but, was a dedicated practitioner and as the main role of the Head of Department was office-based, Alan came in to pull it all together as well as teaching when ever he could.

Boy was that the right move, not just for Brian but, for the many students as well. Alan later said "Brian was the best teacher of Shakespeare he had ever met". A compliment indeed as he was a chief A-level examiner and moderator!

It later was an honour and a privilege, through Alan, to be employed, to actually GET PAID for what was my dream job.

Although as many students would no doubt testify to their cost, my acting skills at being strict in front of them belied my true character at the many 'practical jokes' played, some which to this day, they had no idea 'twas little old me' who set them up. So, confession time later!

But that would be a long time in the future. For now, I am just about to enter the doors of a new world, and about to discover 'HOW COOL WAS BRIAN HINDLE'.

2 - SHOULD I STAY OR SHOULD I GO?

I am sure, nay certain, others have their own life-affirming memories of their time at Clifton Drive Performing Arts and maybe they can be collated for another book but, as far as I can remember accurately, this is an account of my first year then, subsequent highlights of MY OWN wonderful journey through my PERFORMING ARTS YEARS!

In the spring of 1988, I realised I needed a change of my 'daily routine' (you would never in a million years guess what that 'day job' was before going to college).

Music was my first love. From a very young child I loved music, so much so, all I ever wanted to do when leaving school was to be a DJ.

I had built up my own DJ'ing business, which was going quite well.

My first thoughts about going back to college were about categorising the thousands of vinyl singles and CD's that I had collected not just for DJ'ing but, my own personal collection.

I also needed to improve my communication skills. Believe it or not I was quite shy as a young boy (no I didn't think you would!)

I was not one for sitting behind a desk, as Mrs Griffiths observed on my year 8 (or as then, second-year) report at St George's: "Putting Stephen to a desk is like putting a sparrow in a cage!" Charming, but true!

So, I looked in to what courses the college had to offer in 'Basic IT' and if there were any complementary communication courses.

I found to my delight, that if I went to college as a full-time student, I could get a grant but, I would have to choose other topics to study to make up a full-time table.

One choice was easy, media studies. Something I felt I had an interest in. The other subject I chose, came to be one of the best decisions I have ever made... PERFORMING ARTS. What better way than to 'get me out of my shell'

Little did I know at the time what I was letting myself in for and how this would have such a dramatic effect on my life in so many different ways (and still does!).

To be honest, I had no idea what world I was about to step into (step being the operative word!).

Let me set the scene.

Location: Clifton Drive South, St Anne's

Blackpool and The Fylde College, School of Performing Arts

It's the second Monday in September 1988, 9.15 a.m.

What seemed like a crowd of football hooligans milling around in what appeared to be a theatre! Surely, I must be in the wrong room? I wasn't!

What I had failed to grasp at enrolment was, this was a full-time Performing Arts Course with a couple of hours per week devoted to media and (what I had wanted to study) I.T Skills.

As The Clash once said: should I stay or should I go?

I decided, for the day at least, I'd 'give it a go'. The good thing being once the noise had been reduced to dull roar, I could see that there was another chap who also shaved and we sort of made a beeline to one another.

A nod to one another gave me the feeling that this gentleman (gentleman huh!) had also been duped into being here but, after a quick introduction and a plan of action we bonded right away and what's more we both had an ally!

From that day until the he died, we stayed in touch. He went on to be a great actor and had a prominent role in the TV series *Dalziel and Pascoe* as Wieldy. Little did we know that day, what lay ahead.

He was used to a much stricter regime having just come out of the army, but like me we gritted our teeth and got on with all the delights of the first day back at school!

Towards the end of that traumatic first day we were informed by a lovely well-spoken gentleman, Head of

Drama Brian Hindle, that the next day we would all be descending on Williamsons Park in Lancaster. "Bring a packed lunch, wear some old outdoor clothing and be prepared to join in the tasks". The coach would depart the college at 9 a.m. prompt!

Foolishly, and I do regret this, I didn't go on the coach, instead choosing to drive up in my own car. I realised, too late, that the coach journey, there and back, was part of the 'getting to know you' so important in performing arts if one is to really open up with your feelings and emotions, especially in that all important introductory induction!

Nevertheless, by the end of the day it had certainly been a real eye opener as to what the course was going to be like.

As an icebreaker, we started with a game of cat and mouse trying to run down lines of people until the command of 'change direction' came.

Then (and this was Jim Thomas's idea) a game of three-legged football. Me a grown mature man, well a bit older at least, playing children's games, legging up students and seeing them roll down that steep hill. Hilarious!

Just before lunch we were randomly put into smaller performance groups and asked, using the wonderful setting of the park, to come up with a short piece to perform to the other groups and staff. Talk about cringeworthy!

We did perform and I got through it but, just before the end of the day, Dave and I had a little chat and made a pact that although it wasn't what we were expecting, we would both give it six weeks. Dave stayed for two years and I stayed for fourteen years!

I can't pretend I enjoyed induction week or, some of the 'drama warm up games' subsequently deployed as the term progressed!

I was still a little shy about letting go of my emotions; more bothered about how my peers would perceive me and not keen on making a fool of myself in front of them.

At first, because of my inhibitions, I particularly disliked one of Angela Moran's go-to parlour games, instances, or to give it its proper title, Improvisation, better known to those in the business, as IMPROV lovie.

Two performers are given a subject to ad lib on. An example could be, say, a setting in a shop when a customer asks for a loaf of bread to which comes the reply from the shop assistant… 'this is a chemist, madam'.

The ad lib goes, on until Angela Moran would clap her hands, one actor would depart and another quickly came in with another completely random line… Talk about thinking on your feet, at the slightest hesitation you were off and the next person was in!

Truth be told, in performing arts (as in life itself I suppose) 'tis better to meet your demons head on and confront them. No room for inhibitions or embarrassment in this profession. I was later to learn about Dave at drama school in a much worse way having to confront this. More of which later!

So, thank you Angela for that life lesson!

I remember one of Brian's in which we all had a 'character from history' written on a label and stuck, with our eyes closed, on our forehead. Not knowing who this character was we then had to ask one question in turn of each group member i.e. is the character male/female king/queen young/old. I asked what my character was famous for? Staying in a lot, came the reply! Turned out I was Ann Frank!

Eventually, because of the size of the intake we were spilt into three different first year groups.

I can't tell you how lucky I was in having such a kind warm-hearted sincere tutor as Angela Hudson. She really was, and is, a lovely person. Thirty-three years later I am still in touch and we meet once a month, along with Jim and Debbie, who you will hear about soon!

I can also remember all my fellow group members of 1c… Let's see.

As well as myself, fortunately (for all of us) the aforementioned Dave, Steve C and Wayne W made up the lads.

It is inevitable in performing arts, maybe because in secondary school, Drama is considered by the boys to be 'cissy' and not macho, that there always seems more girls than boys, which does lead to an imbalance of roles!

So yes, inevitably more girls than boys. Think this is the full list who, suffered the slings and arrows of outrageous fortune, having to endure my presence. Cecilia, who I think left the course early, Liz, Lorna, Donna, Andrea, Helen, Kim and Katy made up the girls, although I think (shoe box) Denise was also in our group (will explain the shoe box reference later!)

The course was multi-faceted. Which for me, meant all my insecurities were laid bare for all to see, especially in my ballet attire! Yes, little old me trying ballet! What a sight! Debbie Smythe was a brilliant dance teacher, so supportive and understanding of Dave and I in our Ballet Dangling outfits, as well as our inadequacies in movement.!

Another area of concern for public humiliation was singing. There had been an incident at junior school which had left me in no doubt at all that my singing should be confined entirely to the privacy of the shower.

Mr Hall, the headmaster then at Stanley Juniors, was a devout Gilbert and Sullivan fan, so in our final year he staged *HMS Pinafore* for which I was one of the butch sailor types (don't laugh) During rehearsal one day someone was singing off key.

"Who's making that dreadful noise!" shouted Mr Hall.

"Bradshaw!" shouted one of my fellow sailors.

"Out, Bradshaw, get out now."

Sulking down the long corridor I heard the singing re-commence, the discordant voice, it's still there! then, he booming voice of Mr Hall rang out again!

"Bradshaw, get back here."

So, as you can imagine, not the most confident of singers!

I have kept in touch with one of two from my days at performing arts which, I have become lifelong friends of, none more so than, the extremely talented person, who was the Head of Music, the one and only Mr Jim Thomas.

Jim had his work cut out to gain my confidence in my singing ability. I still have a lousy singing voice but because of Jim, who said "Everybody can sing!" I am now confident enough to inflict much pain and suffering on whoever is within earshot!

Music was my first love and it will be my last! So, I was fascinated on a Friday morning to have printed lyrics from so many different genres of music, from musical theatre, classic pop songs, folk and contemporary songs.

Jim sought to broaden our musical repertoire. The aspect that fascinated me however was, that, these songs I had heard on the radio all those years ago, how, in almost each one, I had misheard the lyrics.

Take Bohemian Rhapsody for example. *Beelzebub got a devil put aside for me.*

I always thought it was, *Beelzebub got a sideboard for me*! Stupid boy!

Although in singing and dance I was a reluctant participant in, drama I was up for!

I cannot tell you how lucky the college was to have, not only one of the best drama teachers in the country but, for me, in Brian, one of the most exemplary human beings I have ever met in my life!

His lessons were a joy to behold. We had a bash at Shakespeare, Restoration Comedy, Commedia Dell'arte (I had to spell check that one) Stanislavski (good old Stan) in fact all styles of theatre were covered in what on paper, could look pretty heavy going and boring.

Brian seemed to bring a dawning and realisation that the world of performing arts was indeed an Aladdin's cave waiting to be plundered and the quench for learning had for me, had never been so great.

Before the 'main event' we always did a warm up or icebreaker. These were great fun, especially the tongue twisters like:

I saw Susie sitting in a shoe shine shop. She sits and shines and shines and sits, sitting in her shoe shine shop.
Peter Piper picked a peck of pickled pepper.

We usually had the whole afternoon to develop whatever Brian had planned and almost without exception it was for me, mind-blowing. Yes, in other classes and lessons there was a certain amount of, shall I say tomfoolery, but in Brian's lessons a desire to learn which brought to the group, discipline.

One anecdote I remember Brian beautifully portraying about 'The Method Style' (or Stan as Laskie) concerned the renowned actor of stage and screen John Gielgud and fresh out of drama school, then a young aspiring actor by the name of Dustin Hoffmann.

Brian said, Dustin had to come onto stage out of breathe and deliver the line "Sire I bring you urgent news from The King" Dustin decided to add a touch of realism to this delivery and ran round the block of the theatre (in costume).

Having done this, he came through the stage door, straight on stage and delivered his line to John Gielgud, "Sire" (pause). "Sire" (longer pause). To which John Gielgud replied, "Is that an urgent message from the king you bring me?"

Apparently afterwards John proffered Dustin a little advice: "It is the actor's role to deliver the lines and not fall over the furniture!" Brilliant!

Brian had his own 'party pieces' No one did Dame Edith Evans like him. I can still hear him now, 'A handbag'. His Kenneth Williams was also exceptional!

As well as two other first year groups there were also two second year groups with some exceptionally talented students, not just the ones like John S and Craig K who, went on to have very successful careers in performing arts. That whole year group seemed to thieve off one another.

Brian was dedicated to helping each student achieve their potential, even going that extra mile in helping them reach it.

I also mentioned at the start my original desire to learn new computer skills.

For Information Technology we had a lady called Carol Nash who had a very dry sense of humour. Craig K and Claire H were good fun in this group. Oh how we laughed back in those early computer days when the main server went down and all our work was lost!

At least I learned to be calm and relaxed when three hours of work has gone down the drain.

The main reason I first came to college was to learn how to categorise my music on database and to this objective my goal was achieved so, thank you, Carol.

Media studies with Ann Nixon and Kay Keir gave me a valuable insight into how the media operated, which included budgeting for mainstream film, storyboarding and what all those hundreds of people on the end credits of films actually did! I am now aware exactly who a 'key grip' is and the one that always amused me, 'best boy' (not what you are thinking, madam!).

Although there were drama students who did Computer Studies, the majority opted for this related subject. One such person was one of my early adversaries. She was, in my eyes, a rather forward young lady (well one out of three isn't bad; she was at least still young). She had the look of Kate Bush and her own (to this day) unique sense of humour. Her thinking-out-loud moments were equally amusing and cringeworthy but always entertaining!

Later, Kaye set up a Journalism Course which I enrolled for. This was a tremendous asset to me as Radio Wave came a-calling for students to get involved. John Barnett, the founder of the Fylde Coast's first independent station, invited me in for a look round and I ended up staying there for twenty-eight years. I seemed to have formed a habit of outstaying my welcome at places, but that's another story (and possibly another book!) although my college and Radio Wave years ran concurrently for over TEN YEARS!

To get back to Kaye, I have a lot to thank her for. Sadly she is no longer with us but some of my fundamental learning around journalism techniques including political law, varying interview styles, the long-lost art of short hand and just opening my mind to new idea's came from her. As a child my grammer and smellings were a tro shus. I used to spell officiate – a fish e ate!

Even later when I became a tutor in Performing Arts, our paths crossed again, enrolling for my professional teaching qualification (PGCE) Kaye was key in my development. The English Language is full of pitfalls in learning punctuation, spelling and grammar. This was, for me a nightmare.

One of the things I remember learning from her was how to punctuate a sentence that we spent ages with:

A panda eats shoots and leaves.

Oh, the joy!

Thank you, Kaye.

Back to performing arts. As I have outlined, the foundation of the course lies within the strength of the wonderful staff. They all had individual talents. Each week Angela Moran, Angela Hudson, Debbie Smythe, Jim Thomas and of course Brian Hindle, gave us the benefit of their vast experience.

Who could forget floating down a stream with Angela Moran, warm ups with Debbie, Jim's singing lessons, helping Angela Hudson find her car that she had parked somewhere around St Anne's YMCA and of course Brian's inspirational drama lessons?

Our group tutor was Angela Hudson. Don't let that quiet and low-key approach fool you, here was a formidable drama teacher and one who has done so much, not only for me but for countless students over many years. I can't thank her enough for all she helped me achieve.

In class we worked well together and in that first year presented some excellent pieces for the weekly coming together of all the groups and years, the Thursday tutorial!

One piece early on Angela directed with skill, was a very challenging piece where, we left it to the audience to decide whether a character was guilty or innocent of a serious crime.

Now bear in mind our first-year group comprised mainly of students that were sixteen or seventeen years of age. The subject in question was rape. As I remember the main characters involved were, the defendant (Dave), the victim (Katy), the prosecution and defence lawyers (Donna and Andrea) and the rest of us playing the judge, and various witnesses called to give evidence.

Two sides of the story were given as to the events of when the alleged crime was committed. The judge then asked the audience (as the jury) to deliver their verdict! Challenging, but rewarding in provoking strong debate and discussion. Theatre in education at its best!

Before we knew it the first term had flown by, and although Dave and I had made a pact to 'see how it went after six weeks', not a word was ever mentioned again, as we both had settled into the varied course.

I got to know Dave quite well as, at that time, he was living just round the corner from me and I gave him a lift in. On those journeys we talked about everything from the course to world politics, but one thing that stuck in my mind was his time spent in the armed forces.

I can't remember for sure now, exactly how long he served but I do remember vividly him saying how much ridicule amounting to bullying, especially by his superior officers, he received.

When he asked to leave he had to declare why, where and what he intended to do. He told them he was going to take a drama course he received the full weight of army prejudice against him, calling him derogatory names, trying to undermine him, making his final weeks intolerable.

He being Dave, got on with it and took it on the chin, but it left a bitter taste, despite all the character building and discipline the army has to offer!

So, we gave it a go, even extremes like singing and dance.

Seeing Dave and I in ballet attire, assuming the four positions, will I'm sure be a memory that will be emblazoned on poor Debs forever! More like ballet danglers than dancers!

One of our first-class projects with Angela Hudson I remember was *Under Milk Wood* by Dylan Thomas. This for me was an extremely challenging play to perform. It was almost spoke in the old 'iambic pentameter' (don't ask!).

Angela's unique 'understated' direction was key to our learning dialogue and portraying character traits.

The group also took on 'non-performance' roles; one of mine was the soundtrack and sound effects.

These effects were key to the success of the production. The first sound effect I had to play was of 'the sea gently lapping on the shore'. Unfortunately, I played track 2 instead of track 3.

Cue 'LOUD whistle of train entering tunnel'! Heart attacks all round. Complete accident, honest!

The next one wasn't, 'and the gentle chimes of the village clock as it struck three'. I searched high and low for an appropriate gentle clock chime. Right on cue, full blast, Big Ben struck three. Certainly woke everyone up!

Happy to report the mishaps with the sound effects were only at dress rehearsal and the performance in tutorial I think, went almost without a hitch.

By now we were approaching the end of the first term. We were informed that there was going to be, on the final day of term, the Christmas Review. It was a mixture of student-devised items and a carol concert. This was to be viewed by the great and the good (the college hierarchy) and the rest of all students and staff studying at Clifton Drive.

It was one of many 'corner stones' of the performing arts calendar. Jim organised the carol concert whilst auditions were invited for the review. The auditions would be in front of our peers, I think mainly second year students.

I'm sure in our that first year we auditioned 'The Nativity' A sketch in which we played primary school children who were not on message, leading to a farcical Nativity.

One line I remember, Mary and Joseph knocking on the inn keeper's door and asking if there was any room at the inn and I think it was Steve C saying, 'yes come in, plenty of room here!' Off stage voice shouting, 'no, no, there's NO room at the inn!'

We failed the audition, but, undeterred, we lapped up the end of term fun.

Every year without fail, Jim Thomas invited assembled guests from all campuses, including the principalship, to "get their car keys out and rattle them for Jingle Bells" such merry japes as we all joined together for a great 'end of term' celebration!

Dave and I had made it to the end of term. He even joined in some of the 'social gatherings' certainly more than I did. Due to my nocturnal DJ'ing, I missed out on those 'quiet little get-togethers' although I did attend a party once at Darren McN house. For some reason I seem to remember Cher W out in the street upsetting the neighbours at some unearthly hour!

Over the years pictures have emerged on social media to suggest, that 'the gatherings' were a little livelier than I was led to believe!

Apart from the musical offering 'The Boyfriend' which, regrettably Dave and I both opted out of, we both now felt, completely emersed and intricated on the course.

Just imagine if on that first day when we met, we both decided that it wasn't for us.

After that sceptical start, we were off and running but, the adventure of a lifetime was only just beginning!

3 – LONDON CALLING!

As well as the Christmas Review, there were, back in the day, several defining points in the performing arts calendar the next of which was the infamous London trip! Stand by for action!

When returning after the Christmas break, anticipation was running high because, at the end of January '89, the Performing Arts Course was off on a theatre visit to London.

The pinnacle of our profession, the West End Stage. The ambition of all performers surely, was to reach and maybe, just maybe, one day to perform there, but for now a visit was still some achievement!

For some students not only was it the first time they had an opportunity to go to London but for some, the first time they had been away from home without their parents. A big responsibility that the college undertook but, if these young aspiring students were to achieve their potential, they had to witness first hand, the pinnacle of their profession!

One cold and frosty morning at the end of January, 6.30 a.m. to be precise, the adventure began. No one was late that day!

The sense of anticipation onboard as we neared The Royal National Hotel was palpable but, what the staff were thinking in letting sixty performing arts students loose in London I do not know. Poor Jim Thomas, Angela Moran and I think, our costume lady, the one and only Wendy Schwarzkachel, of which more later!

Jim and Angela advised us that in Leicester Square there was a half-price ticket booth (and me thinks still is!) where, upon queuing, excess theatre tickets can be purchased for erm, half price!

Dave and I shared a room and headed off out to see what was on offer.

Noel Cowards, The Vortex with Mira Aiken and a new fresh-faced actor called Rupert Everett, were amongst a strong cast. What could possibly go wrong?

Well almost everything was the answer. It was 'preview night' so the great and the good of theatre-land critics were in attendance

On arrival, we noted that Ruby Wax was seated in the row in front. Dress-wise, dinner suits and ball gowns were the main order of the day, so you can imagine what others must have thought when two scruffy gits turned up in the posh dress circle seats in jeans!

The main curtain was up and a mesh cloth allowed us to glimpse a dinner party with the cast already in action.

Cue lights, now, just the two main actors on stage. Gorse mesh curtain rises. Rupert stands and with silver cigarette case in hand, makes his way over to Mira spread on a 'Chaise longue', he trips over the edge of the rug and the case, full of cigs are scattered all over the set, causing Mira to rise, first her eyebrows then, her rear-end from where she was lead to join Rupert on all fours, gathering in the cigs, whilst delivering their lines!

That was just the start of the fun! Half way through Act One Mira alone on stage contemplating her thoughts. Her beautiful authentic phone rings. Three rings and she answers it, oh hello, only for the blooming thing to carry on ringing!

Well, her stare to the audience could have killed! Pity the poor Stage Manager at the interval!

At the interval the gorse fell, once again a cocktail party ensued, lights dimmed, cue curtain. Did the mesh curtain rise? rise it did not! The mesh curtain remained down until mid-way through the second half when it eventually raised to a big cheer and clap!

Many years later a popular play I think was based on this opening night of the Vortex called, *The Play That Goes Wrong*!

I couldn't wait to see the *Evening Standard* the following day for their review! Sure enough, there it was in black and white 'Opening Night Disaster'. In a perverse sort of way I took great pleasure in that as I thought, well if pros can 'cock it up' then little old me 'drying' isn't so bad!

Jim used to describe breakfast, at The Royal National as "As much toast as you could eat" after which we embarked, the following day, on the freedom of London!

Most of our group who were on the visit, went out together and I remember an incident at the world-famous wax museum.

I think this time, Dave's brainwave, when after looking round and before leaving Madame Tussauds we had the obligatory group pic on the foyer bench. Dave then suggested we pose as a wax work group, keep still and don't move! Sure enough, a party of Japanese tourists decided to take a closer look at the this 'life-like' wax work (although why they thought a group of students would make a good wax work I do not know). BOO! Oh my goodness, what a shock they and the rest of the assembled crowd got.

We felt good about our first public performance as we were escorted from the premises by security!

That evening I chose to go it alone to see my favourite author's play *The Mouse Trap.*, the world's longest running production! From a young boy I have been a big fan of Agatha Christie. One book in particular, *The Murder of Roger Ackroyd* is probably the best book I have ever read, so I had a heightened sense of expectation to see this production.

I have since learnt, on my many subsequent theatre visits, not to have any expectations whatso ever, other than to open one's mind, ears and eyes to what is on offer.

As you have probably guessed from the last paragraph, *The Mouse Trap* was a huge disappointment and 'who done it' was not hard, for an Agatha aficionado, to work out 'who done it' but besides that the plot was plodding and (in my humble opinion) not particularly 'well-acted'.

Oh well, never mind, the night was young and tomorrow we would be heading back up North!

Although 'on my tod' and a big boy now, I set off into the London night to see what was 'on offer'.

The famous Hippodrome Night Club in the heart of London seemed like a great way to finish the evening off. Live on stage, Boney M.! What could possibly go wrong?

Again, little did I know when paying my 'fiver' to get in, exactly what could and DID go wrong that evening!

Dave Cash, he of Kenny Everett stable, a then Capital Radio DJ, hosted the evening. As an 'ice breaker' he invited audience members on stage for some fun games. Hold that thought in mind!

Dave then introduced Boney M., big build up, before, on a hydraulic lift, up they popped. Unlike the play I had NO expectations of Boney M., so was pleasantly surprised at how flipping good they were. The joint was jumping and a good time was had by all!

After their great performance they stood on their hydraulic lift and descended. On came Dave Cash and (in the days of being able to smoke indoors) and said "I'll give £10 to the first person on stage with a lighted cigarette"

First out of the blocks, was a young girl in a short white dress and high heels who ran towards him with said lighted cig. Have you guessed what happened?

The poor girl tripped and fell thirty feet down the still lowered hydraulic lift that had taken Boney M. down but, hadn't been returned up. A stunned silence descended on the packed crowd!

In what seemed an eternity, when time seemed to stand still, the ambulance arrived and an announcement was made for all to calmly and slowly leave. Some people were crying and visibly upset from what they had just witnessed. I left the Hippodrome that night not knowing whether the young girl was dead or alive!

When I got back to the hotel I went straight up to my room, switching on the radio hoping to hear of her fate, but fearing the worst!

It wasn't until the following day when, once again in the good old *London Standard* I read, not on the front page, but tucked away in the inner pages: 'Girl breaks both her legs in club fall'. At least I knew she was actually alive, thank goodness!

This was to be the first of several memorable London visits.

There was still time for an amusing foot note to end our first London visit on! at least for Dave and I.

Two girls, who shall remain nameless, let's call them, for argument's sake Katy N and Helen D, thought it would be an amusing idea, when Dave and I were 'nodding off, to call us on the hotel internal phone, not once but, several times during the night Eventually, it did stop. Dave and I vowed revenge!

Being ex-army, Dave was an early riser so, at 6 a.m. we returned the compliment, pretending to be the hotel reception. I phoned their room, advising the girls that 'check out' was 6.30 a.m. They would need to be packed and ready in reception for then. Bleary-eyed and none too communitive, one of them muttered something incoherent, then the phone went dead!

We both headed down to the restaurant and took our place but, hidden from view. Sure enough, on the dot of 6.30, down they came, coats on, suitcase in hand, puzzled as to why they were the only people in reception at that unearthly hour.

It wasn't until we had set off back on the coach, that Dave and I confessed to the hoax call. Their faces were a picture!

So endeth an eventful first London trip, but there would be many more adventures to come and lots more exploits!

4 – *BRIGHT LIGHTS* (or, now where did I put them dungarees?)

Back at college, Wednesday afternoons were set aside for show rehearsals. During the course of the year, the college had two performance slots booked at the beautiful Grand Theatre, the first of which was a 'one night only' showcase event which, enabled not only students to show off their individual talents but collectively, with routines devised through class work in all aspects of the course!

This production was of course, BRIGHT LIGHTS! Da da da Bright Lights! Performed at the Grand Theatre on Sunday 19th Feb 1989

Quite a big part of the production was dancing and singing' to which Dave and I politely declined the offer, especially when knowing essential dress code was dungarees!

Angela Hudson had been working with our group in class on, *T.S Eliot's Old Possum's Book of Practical Cats* This was to be our groups contribution to *Bright Lights*. A polished piece, directed and set beautifully by Angela.

On the night, the performance went well. I have to say, for me, Wayne W was stand out in his top hat and tails whilst, another student uttered the immortal line of 'and how would you address a cat' making the whole piece come to life!

As well as *'Cats'* the other contributions I remember were, *Riptide, London Town* and *Daisy Pulls It Off*.

Dave and I also took part in the finale, which was that year's big hit ballad, *'The Living Years'*. The entire course on stage, John S up front and centre, giving it wallop. I think we did it justice!

Bright Lights took place on a Sunday evening. You can imagine the 'euphoric high' from the first-year students at least, coming off stage thinking this was just the start of their journey into a career in performing arts! I think the second-year students were a little more astute having performed at the Grand the previous year especially in the highly acclaimed *West Side Story*.

That year, we were lucky to also perform *Bright Lights* the following Sunday, March 8th at The Charter Theatre in Preston. To be honest I don't remember to much about it apart from a couple of stand-out things.

When our group were called to the stage to perform our '*Cats*' excerpt, in full costume, we had to go up a flight of stairs. Unfortunately, one of our group, who by that time should have known me better, asked me directions to the stage, as she needed to finish her makeup. Now fancy asking me!

"Yes, it's up two flights of stairs," I said.

Opening the door at the top of two flights of stairs, she only walked out into the dress circle in full costume. Not sure who was most shocked: the audience or, the mortified Kim S!

The other one was a solo singer who, just before going on stage lost her radio mic down the top of her performance gown, pulling her gown down to retrieve it and asking me (nervously and shaking) to reattach it and, without missing a beat, she said "It's a good job I don't have any inhibitions!" What a true pro! Glass of water for Mr Bradshaw though!

5 – LAMDA EXAMS, oh ek!

Back at college the following morning, there was no time to rest on our laurels as the following week the dreaded LAMDA exams were upon us!

For these exams we had to choose three suitable contrasting pieces of text from stage plays, learn and polish them, before performing in front of one of the country's top LAMDA examiners, who just happened to be Brian Hindle!

No favours here, there were strict criteria to be adhered to.

If there was an adrenalin rush for our Grand Theatre performances there was a palpable sense of nervousness, especially amongst first years and particularly in one first year, NAMELY ME!

Cool I was not! On the day of my exam, Thursday 16th March at 1.15 p.m. I can't tell you how nervous I was, what an ordeal for me to perform solo pieces in front of Brian!

From memory my three pieces were *Hobson's Choice*, *Brief Encounter* and *The Wilmslow Boy*.

Hobson's Choice was my comic piece, by far the one I performed best, this sandwiched in-between two contrasting serious pieces. Would my nerves get the better of me? But more than that, had Brian been convinced of my performances?

The sense of achievement when Brian told me I had passed, I wanted to hug him! My mark was 117, which wasn't brilliant, but for me it meant everything!

I hadn't let Angela Hudson down who spent her own time in rehearsing and polishing them with me. Thank you!

6 – MY BOYFRIEND EXPERIENCE!

After the trauma of LAMDA exams, it was full steam ahead with the annual Grand Theatre musical. The previous year's show was *West Side Story*, acknowledged now as one of the best ever performed by college students at The Grand.

In fairness, *West Side Story* had everything going for it. It was widely regarded anyway, as one of the 'all-time great musicals', add to that, not only, was it the ideal vehicle for a student production but, in that production, there lay a wealth of 'potentially' great talent, including John S, so no pressure then for this year's students to come up with the goods!

What better than, the choice of *The Boyfriend* for our follow up production. Well to be honest, quite a lot!

At first it was greeted with a little scepticism, on the basis no-one had heard of it!

Rehearsals for Sandy Wilson's *The Boyfriend* took place on Wednesday afternoons mainly in spring and summer terms.

Dave and I took 'the fifth' but were more than happy to help out back stage.

It was a difficult production for anyone, let alone students to get to grips with, as it was so stylised, but as performance time approached the production came together under the expert direction of Angela Moran.

The Grand Theatre Blackpool, designed by Frank Macham is acknowledged as one of the most beautiful theatres in the world. What a privilege then to have this great opportunity to perform there.

We had great fun with the publicity shots, using the interior and exterior of The Grand Hotel (no relation to The Grand Theatre) situated behind our college. Looking back the shots in the vintage car, were some of the best ever for a college production.

Excitement mounted on arrival for our Grand Theatre run from the 23rd-27th May 1989 as dress rehearsal began.

What an amazing achievement to see the stage, set and cast in their costumes!

One person, besides Angela, who in deserves credit for the success of this production is the one and only Wendy Schwarzkachel, wardrobe mistress extraordinaire!

Come curtain up, nerves and expectation were palpable and most got through without bumping into the furniture!

As anyone who has performed in any production, amateur or professional, small church hall or Grand Theatre, there is nothing like the acclaim of an audience and the euphoria when the curtain comes down. Multiply that ten-fold and you get some sense of achievement after that first night performance, which was quickly brought down to earth by the director, Angels M, asking the cast to "please stay on stage for 'notes!'

One thing the production didn't need was a pillock back stage playing practical jokes.

I now realise just how un-professional SOME of these were including, both I did during the Wednesday matinee.

Early on in the performance a chorus line was waiting backstage to go on but, had to endure, for what seemed like an eternity, a 'horrendous stench' from a strategically placed stink bomb! "I think I'm going to be sick" one girl shouted before gritting her teeth, then smiling as she went on stage!

That was bad enough, later just before the interval, there was a beautifully set scene on the terrace which ended with a couple exiting through the French Window's or so they hoped! There was poor Wayne W and partner, stuck on stage, tugging at the door, trying but failing to open it. Unsurprisingly really, as earlier I had locked it. "The bloody thing's stuck," he muttered as they hurriedly wondered out through the wings. I unreservedly apologize!

On the final evening we were honoured to have the writer of the play, Sandy Wilson, grace us with his presence. I know Angela Moran was thrilled, if not a little nervous as to what he might think of her directing his play. She needn't have been, as he was ecstatic! Angela was 'over the moon' with his fulsome praise, not just in her direction but getting the performances out of the students in a genre that wasn't easy for them!

I think Angela Moran had somehow managed to persuade Sandy Wilson to 'waver' some of the royalties (maybe over a small G&T) on this musical. Production costs were usually astronomical, at around £10,000, which included theatre hire, set costume, orchestra and production costs, copyright usually was around £1,000. Box office split, also favoured the company i.e. The Grand!

I think Sandy Wilson was overjoyed in us performing it, and so was most gracious and generous in helping to keep costs down.

We had a great principal at St. Anne's in Neville Wakling who, each year, underwrote any losses, justifying it with the learning experiences that students got. Oh boy, was he right! What an experience the students had. Along with the London Theatre Visit, this gave an incentive to achieve, second to none!

Both Brian and Alan, the subsequent Head of Department, said that our students who, later auditioned for prestigious drama schools were thought of highly by those establishments as the reputation in 'foundation' training at college usually ensured a more all-round and grounded student.

A great experience but one I fear John S has not forgiven me for (and I don't blame him!).

A few years later, after establishing himself as an extremely talented all-round performer, he appeared on the cult teatime chat show, *The Priory* hosted by Jamie Theakston.

His persona on this was 'cool and laid back'. Their production company had contacted me, by then I was the Performing Arts Marketing and Publicity Manager and agreed to their request for a copy of *The Boyfriend* which

John took the lead role in. All singing and dancing in a lovely bellboy costume (not cool in the slightest).

After showing clips and bigging John up of his many recent successes, Jamie then dropped him right in it.

"So, John, you've not always exuded this cool persona, have you?"

John's reply, classic, head in hands: "You haven't, have you?"

(Jamie) "Roll VT."

Half the TV screen showing, John, in a cringeworthy excerpt from *The Boyfriend* and half showing him barely able to watch what was being shown.

After the clip John looked straight into the camera and said: "I know who sent you that and I'm coming to get you."

True to word, he did. Fortunately for me, I wasn't around that day but Jim told me he was not best pleased!

Over the years I've followed John's acting career closely and bar none, I think he is the finest actor in the UK. So versatile, so believable in whatever character he plays! Once again though, an apology is in order!

A big problem for the staff was how, after half term, to get sixty odd students back on planet earth after the euphoria of that great experience?

7 – NOT HOME TIME ALREADY

In truth, the summer term up until we finished at the end of June wasn't dramatic. My memories of this wind down were few and far between.

I remember that students who had missed LAMDA exams in March could re-sit them in June.

Angela Hudson had persuaded one of our group, who had missed the original exam, to perform her pieces on stage, in the theatre, in front of our group.

Kim S, quite rightly nervous at performing in front of her peers, lent forward in a period 'low-cut serving wench costume' to announce her piece, with two serving vessels, one in each hand in hand.

Unfortunately, I could not resist.

"Nice jugs, Kim."

Only those who were there will confirm the uproar and laughter which ensued. Quite naturally and correctly Angela sprung to my defence, "Stephen didn't mean it like that!" The students knew better, Stephen did mean it like that!

Glad to say Kim S passed with flying colours!

The other events of note to look back on in the summer term were both social.

A garden party was thrown by Angela Moran which, as I recall, was all very civilized, apart from, Cher, who lived with Angela (although not in the biblical sense) It seemed the entire student population of St Anne's had descended on Angela's back garden that day. Apparently, these gathering were legendary! Hope she had understanding neighbours! Need it with Cher causing mayhem!

Over the course of the year our group had bonded so well, even socialising together. There was even a day trip arranged to the Lake District with Dave, myself and I think,

Katy N, Andrea K and Liz H who, as I recall, had a great sense of humour!

Just a great fun day out with plenty of laughs!

My first year on the Performing Arts Foundation Course had drawn to a close. What an adventure. I can truly say one of the best of my life.

Not only had I achieved what I set out to do, gain competence in I.T, but also thanks to the staff, also gain confidence in my own ability, which helped me perform better at my 'proper job' that of a DJ, host and compere.

As well as Jim, Debs and the Angela's, others played their part in ensuring I not only developed personally but, I also thoroughly enjoyed that first year. Lovely people like Wendy and the academic staff to, including Carol Nash, Kaye Keir, Dave Swan and Mike Woods, who's dry sense of humour wasn't lost on me, and not forgetting Phil Sessions, whom, I occasionally played badminton with at lunch times instead of eating in the canteen hosted by the inevitable (chips with everything) Jenny! Even the little old Liberian lady was a character, but for me BRIAN HINDLE was most definitely COOL!

Not only did I stay longer than six weeks, I now couldn't wait to see what the second year would bring?

At least you won't have to wait as long as I did to find out!

8 – ME, A BIG SECOND YEAR!

September '89 began the start of my second year. I was unaware then of who, out my first-year group would return.

Sad to say several didn't so, the three first year groups from last year were combined into two second year groups. Added into the mix, there was also the odd second-year from last year who came back for a third year. Some just wouldn't leave (I think Dean T still has an entry in the Guinness book of records for the number of years he was there as a student!).

In a way I felt more pressure to achieve in the second year than in the first.

As a new student last year, I thought wow, these second-year students, especially the lads, who I foolishly measured myself against, had set such a high bar that I had not a hope of reaching.

Allied with that now, the new intake, may have expectations on this year's second years, including me!

Now, looking back, I know the second-year group that I looked up to whilst in my first year, were genuinely talented. Some had successfully auditioned for prestigious drama schools in London and I just knew John S would make it big time, such a talented performer, despite his bellboy costume in The Boyfriend.

Once again Brian's classes were a joy and I loved the weekly variety of class work. In truth I don't have the depth of memory to relate as many second-year class experiences as my first.

I do remember undertaking a one-year City and Guilds Journalism course, once again with Kaye Keir and Anne Nixon.

This was to prove invaluable as, unknown to me, thanks to this course and my own driving ambition, I would soon achieve my lifetime ambition of becoming a radio presenter.

That I can tell you is certainly a story worth telling as hopefully, (lawyer's allowing) I fully intend to do so! (Note to self, may have to change the names to protect the guilty!)

One of my fellow students back in those 'halcyon days' was a guy called Chris H. Part way through the course he was successful at applying for a 'junior post' with the Football League whose HQ was not but a pitch length away on Clifton Drive.

He sought my opinion as to whether he should stay on the course or take a risk and take up this potential career opportunity!

He did leave and rose to the heights in the FA and is also a well-known voice in sports journalism. Glad to say I still see him from time to time, the last of which a poignant coincidence, Brian Hindle's funeral, where his sister Clair had asked him to help video the occasion as Brian's brother had arranged for CT Hull Funeral Services to conduct the proceedings.

Despite the sad occasion we were both glad to see one another and for a moment or two relived those far-off happy college days!

9 – ENTER ALAN, CENTRE STAGE

In performing arts, the most dramatic occurrence of the second year, unquestionably, was the arrival of Alan Evans, assuming the mantle of, Head of Performing Arts.

He was to go on and develop the Foundation Drama Course into one of the highest acclaimed Performing Arts centres in the UK.

I cannot speak too highly of his achievements but as you can imagine the thought of change to me, with my limited skills left me anxious as to the what the immediate future held!

Once again, my fears were to be completed unfounded as within a year of his arrival, I found myself (unbelievably) on the payroll.

As I have mentioned earlier, I am pretty confident the appointment of Alan Evans was made with Brian's blessing, giving him time to continue to do what he loved best: teach drama!

I remember to this day my first meeting with Alan. It was mid-way through the first term and our group were rehearsing a World War One piece with Angela Hudson, I think for Armistices Day, on November 11

The tone and content had to be spot on to reflect the magnitude of The Great War. He couldn't have picked a better time to come into The Media Studio in the basement which was our rehearsal space, he walked in to witness Dave in full flow!

The piece was eventually incorporated into a montage for our annual production of *Bright Lights*, and was a highlight of that year's production.

I will detail later how Alan came to make profound changes to the course and take it to, not only to the next level, but eventually to be, one of the most acclaimed

Performance Centre's in the country where our students were looked upon by drama schools as 'rounded'.

Ultimately, it made not a jot of difference as, only the most consummate of auditions ensured progression to one of these prestigious 'centres of excellence'!

10 – FIND ME

Back on course, there was a buzz of anticipation before the announcement of our annual musical.

That soon dissipated on announcement of *The Pajama Game*. There was an initial sense of being 'underwhelmed' and much scratching of heads ensued to find out about this old Doris Day musical.

Once again, I pleaded the fifth but Dave decided to give it a go, especially on finding out his character at least didn't have to perform any song and dance routines!

Casting of the production took place, followed by Wednesday afternoon rehearsals, but there was to be plenty of 'drama' before the staging of this production.

One of the most intriguing plays our second-year group emersed themselves in was, a play by Olwyn Wymark *Find Me.*

Brief synopsis: Based on a true story about a young girl called Verity, who had several different personalities. In fact, I think she was diagnosed with seven different personality traits, but in the play there were five different Veritys. See if I can remember them, course I can I have a script here, in fact two, I seemed to have ended up with Katy's! script (P.S. you are welcome to it back!)

Our five Verity's were Katy N, Jo W, Suzy K, Cher W and Andrea K?

I may be wrong, I usually am. I think we brought various plays to the table to read through but, had to cast with the ratio of group members in mind (i.e. more with the alternative plumbing) I think there might have only been Dave, Steve C and I then about eight or more girls.

It would prove to be both complex and challenging in terms of trying to understand the issues raised.

I seem to recall both Brian, and Alan directed. In a way this helped lend a different dimension as some of their ideas were incorporated into the production.

As Verity grew, along with her issues so, a different performer took over her changing persona.

Although we set a tentative date of March 3rd '90 for a performance in our theatre, we also knew that this production would be an excellent opportunity for 'Theatre in Education', a tour no less!

Where it would take us well, let's see when we come back to this fascinating piece after the Christmas break!

Rehearsals also were underway for our February one night performance at the Grand, *Bright Lights*!

11 – CHRISTMAS WIND!

So, all systems go as, also approaching fast was the Christmas Review 1989!

Feeling a little more confident this year, our group contribution was an outrageous restoration type piece entitled *When the Wind Blows,* named after the mid-eighties holocaust cartoon. Only the title was borrowed, not the subject matter!

It featured Dave as an aging butler and Donna S who, was the 'well-to-do lady of the house', who was throwing a drinks party for her assembled guests, played by the rest of our group.

Every time the aging butler bent over to serve drinks to the posh guests, he broke wind, violently!

Now, ever since I was a young child, from about the age of nine I have this 'uncanny knack' of being able to blow 'loud realistic raspberries' on my hand. I won't bore you with the scientific details but as a child, in shops, on public transport and in 'the gentleman's excuse me', it has caused great amusement!

So, positioning myself in the wings, I 'let rip' every time Dave bent over! Dave was able to stay in character but poor Donna couldn't, corpsing every time I let rip!

I could hear the audience roaring with laughter but, what would the principal and his assembled dignitaries, including the Mayor and Mayoress think? Would my exemplary reputation of 'butter wouldn't melt in his mouth' be tarnished?

On stage I didn't consider myself to be a particularly good actor but off stage I was able to, so far, 'get away with murder', as you are no doubt by now beginning to realise!

I needn't have worried, after the performance, Brian said "that's one the funniest things I've ever seen. You had us all in stitches". Which goes to show, even the Mayoress likes a good old giggle!

My most memorable moment in the Christmas Review however, was still to come the following year, but for now that would do!

12 – ANGELA'S PJ PARTY, RANDY, PETER O'TOOLE AND MY 'TARNISHED REPUTATION'!

As sure as night follows day, the London trip followed the Christmas Review.

London held no fears this time round and although Dave didn't come on this trip, I felt my roommates, P and J. (will explain why only initials shortly) would put up with my antics. What delights did The Royal National hold this year?

As previously mentioned, that year's musical production was to be *The Pajama Game*, so what better than a Pyjama Party in a hotel room? I had photocopied enough invites for all the students, all I needed now on arrival were their room numbers.

You may well ask how such an innocent student could manage to persuade reception staff who had been specifically trained to not, under NO circumstances give out room numbers to students. That rooming list in wrong hands, could wreak havoc!

Part with it they did, so felt pen in hand, a Pyjama Party at midnight, bring a bottle, was arranged in the appropriate room! I posted all the invites under the doors, including one under our own room, so no suspicion could be laid at my door!

On returning from my evening's theatre entertainment, frankly not one I remember, but whatever entertainment it was, it would pale into insignificance by comparison of the 'In house entertainment' that was about to commence!

At around 11.30 I found a suitable place in which to view, what was for the next couple of hours, was to be the best 'farce' in London, for the room I had printed the invites for was, none other than our 'matriarchal leader,' Angela Moran.

What joy it was watching at periodical intervals, students arriving, in their night attire, bottle in hand, knocking on said door, shocked to be greeted by Angela who'd been trying to get to sleep, answering the door in her curlers and negligent!

"What the hell are you playing at, walking the corridors dressed like that? I suppose you think it's funny knocking at my door at gone midnight?"

At one point around ten students, some already the worse for wear, knocked at the door. Poor Angela by this time had had enough, "Who gave you my room number, you've not heard the last of this, just wait till the morning."

Still they came until, the word must have got around and I think the last knock came at about 1.50 a.m.!

Next morning a stream of apologetic students ensured Angela's mood was lifted. As it transpired, that following evening justice was served. My credibility was severely compromised with Angela Moran, through no fault of my own!

To this day, I have never admitted organizing The Pajama Party, so if you were one of the students who knocked on Angela's door that evening, again, apologies!

Now, that following day after a hard slog in HMV, I trundled along to Leicester Square to purchase my half price theatre ticket.

I didn't know too much about the play I chose but, did about its leading performer, an opportunity to see, one of the country great actors, Peter O'Toole in *Geoffrey Bernard Is Unwell*.

A one-man virtuoso performance (whatever that means!) Although the story, by Keith Waterhouse, about a real live journalist left me somewhat nonplus. (Nonplus, what a much under used word that is!)

If, what happened during the interval that evening hadn't occurred, I would have left the Apollo Theatre that night having seen a brilliant actor and performance in a distinctly average' play!

Sometimes life throws up opportunities you just don't expect, or can pass up on. This night was to prove such an occasion, but with consequences that I wouldn't realize until I got back to the hotel!

Buying a 'half price' theatre ticket for one is akin, I should imagine, to going on a 'blind date', but as I never have been on a blind date, maybe the comparison is unfair!

I couldn't fail to be distracted during the first act by the young lady whom I was randomly plonked next to, who was taking notes. "Ah" I thought to myself, "a reviewer". Nearly right!

"I'm sorry for the distraction," the young lady said at the interval. "Oh, don't apologize. It's been more interesting watching you write than the production!" Me and my big mouth!

After exchanging pleasantries, Randy (her name!) informed me that she was an American exchange student and her magazine had set up an interview with Peter O'Toole after the production!

I tried in vain to clarify my negativity but failed miserably, because you can't 'blag a blagger'. She found it most amusing, as I just kept digging myself deeper in it!

We struck up an immediate rapport and realised we both had the same sense of humour, a rare thing for me as I can, with just one word and no brain filter, upset people without even knowing I was doing so or worst still, knowing it was going to cause upset! A trait which, to this very day I still maintain with ease! I am still convinced my sarcasm will one day, cause my ultimate demise!

The fact, as well as studying drama, I also mentioned I was studying journalism was, music to her ears as, she immediately seconded me to come with her and feed her 'reputable' questions to Peter O'Toole. Me and my big mouth again!

More scribbling ensued in the second act, by both of us, but by now my senses were heightened knowing my comments would have to be at least articulate!

We had, after the performance, time to compare notes then, with interview questions in hand we headed for the stage door!

He came out with his trademark fedora on, wearing that cheeky grin you can picture him with. A delight to interview, he put Randy at ease and before we knew it half an hour had passed without me incurring any black eyes. The interview came to end, but not before I got the obligatory signed programme, which, to this day I still have!.

That interview was not the last I was to have with an 'A list celeb' as several years later I wangled an interview with Gene Wilder who was starring in *Laughter on the 23rd Floor*' about a famous group of script writers who wrote for Sid Caesar's *Your Show of Shows*.

Those were no ordinary script writers; some went on to be the most famous names in American Comedy. They included Woody Allen, Mel Brooks, Carl Reiner, Neil Simon and Larry Gelbart (M*A*S*H)

After Peter O'Toole had left, we looked at one-another, having only met a couple of hours earlier, in disbelief at what had happened, not just doing the interview but how laid back and easy it was!

Her deadline was midnight, so we rushed back to her flat, writing a thousand-word interview that was dispatched with minutes to spare. A quick glass of red wine to celebrate our achievement was downed, before I ordered a taxi back to the hotel. (Honest.)

Our first meeting was also to be our last, although we stayed in touch by, ironically writing, we never actually met again although I was invited out to Boston.

In truth I should have stayed the night on Randy's sofa as, what happened (besides being ripped off by the taxi driver) back at the hotel, was unbelievable. Should have written it up and sent it to Ray Cooney! (If unaware of whom be he, please feel free to look him up!)

I arrived back at the hotel at gone 1a.m. Picking up my key from a deserted reception, all I wanted was my bed, so

I entered the lift, pressed the desired button and thought, not long now before my poor little head could hit the pillow, ah, sleep, per chance to dream!

When the lift door opened, I heard this kerfuffle, oh ek I thought, please not our lot!... It was, and what was worse, right outside my room!

Now let me say here and now, if I had been sharing with Dave again, what followed would never have happened.

Dave hadn't come on this London trip, so I was sharing with J and P

I am loathed to name names as people's lives have moved on. So, for this 'steamy bit' initials will suffice!

P had gone to stay with D overnight who, he met at college last year, before she moved down to London, fine!

That gave J and D, in my absence, an opportunity to 'get to know one another better' so, let's just say, in that room on that night, young love had blossomed!

Putting the key in the door and just about to turn it, giggles from the assembled girls outside heightened my senses. The conversation went something like this:

Karen R: (one of the gigglers outside) "Don't go in."

Me: "And why."

K: "J and D are in there."

Me: "OK."

So, I politely knocked on my own door!

J: "Who is it?"

Me: "Only Steve, your roommate. Can I come in?"

J: "Er no. I didn't think you were coming back so D and I are 'spending the night together'. Can you sleep elsewhere?"

Me: "Bit awkward, not got anywhere else."

J: "Could you sleep in reception."

Me: (complete silence!)

Me: "Yes, OK, J. No worries, have fun, goodnight."

To my surprise, both J and D said goodnight. It's what you do for friends, isn't it! Isn't it?

There was still half a dozen or so students outside my room.

"Steve, where will you sleep?" one asked.

"Not a clue," came the reply. Then, that lightbulb moment which seemed so logical!

"Why don't you sleep in D's bed," said one of the two Sarah's, who D was sharing with.

Sarah 2 agreed, adding, "Yes, she won't be needing it!"

It seemed the logical answer, didn't it? A free bed, instead of a disturbed night's sleep in reception?

I don't really think in accepting that kind offer of a bed for the night, I quite realised just what the repercussions would have for all concerned, especially my untarnished reputation with the staff!

Let me say from the outset that when the door shut on the young ladies' room, I did not for one second consider what, naively, I had agreed to!

Hindsight is a wonderful thing, if only I had plumped for hotel reception!

The two Sarah's, as I will refer to them as for the purpose of the narrative, Sarah 1 and Sarah 2, were really kind and accommodating (no cheap quips please). Both were in their night attire, me fully dressed in my going out clothes with, not only no nightwear, but not even a toothbrush!

Still, sleeping in my trollies would be fine; just a bed was all I craved!

Now at this point, despite me setting the scene as to what could in some people's minds turn into a, how can I put it politely? Well, I'm sure you know as to what I refer, but, that thought NEVER crossed my mind, well hardly ever, (a G&S HMS Pinafore line!) instead, I undressed in the dark, slipped under the covers and due to the night's exertions, fell asleep in the wink of an eye. (Honest!)

I was, however, awoken in the middle of the night by a very loud scream!

Sarah 2 had got up to use the loo (that rhymed!). I stayed put but Sarah 1 went to investigate. They both came out screaming.

"There's a massive spider in the bath!" screamed Sarah 2. "Steve, Steve, you've got to get rid of it!" said Sarah 2.

Throwing back the sheets and springing into action immediately, for this was an emergency of epic proportions, I had not considered my state of attire!

Their state of panic turned to one of uncontrollable laughter, as my designer 'Y-Fronts' were being modelled by my good self, It wasn't then, or has have ever been, 'a pretty sight!'

No time to lose, grabbing the obligatory hotel glass I placed it over the spider, hand over the top of the glass, ran to the door, stepped into the corridor and emptied said spider onto the carpet, which quickly made its escape. CLICK, the door had shut behind me. I'm outside in my trollies knocking on the door of two female students shouting "LET ME IN!" at goodness knows what hour in the morning!

More to the point, what the occupants of adjoining rooms, including some fellow students, would have made of my loud demands, I don't know! I'm just thankful none came to their doors to find out!

Thankfully the door was answered, which prompted another fit of laughter as they gazed at my choice of undergarments. Personally, the old 'harvest festivals' have always been my preferred choice. Too much information I hear you say!

We did stay up chatting for a while, as it was difficult for them to maintain their composure having witnessed the double horror of not only a giant (miniature) spider but the hideous sight of my choice of trollies!

They could have conquered their arachnophobia fear in later life but, the ghastly site of me in my Y fronts will have probably scarred them for life!

We eventually got off but the events of the that whole evening would live long in the memory.

From O'Toole too Y-Fronts (please fill in own punchline!)

D returned to her room the following morning and I to mine. What was said between them, I know not!

What I did know was checkout was imminent and after as much toast as we could eat, we were back on the coach!

Angela Moran was slowing making her way down the coach doing a register check. I was sat with my newspaper in front of me reading the review of the show I had seen the previous night. The two Sarah's were sat in the seat in front of me. When Angela reached them, the conversation went something like this:

Angela: "Good morning, girls, everything all right last night?"

Sarah 1: "Yes, apart from D not sleeping in our room."

Angela: "Oh, where did she sleep then?"

Sarah 1: "With J!"

Angela: "WHAT! Who was J sharing with?"

Sarah 2: "Er, P and Steve but P didn't come back, he stayed at his girlfriend's."

Angela: "Oh he did, did he?" (I glanced at her raised eyebrows from over my paper, which was still firmly covering my face!)

Angela: "And what about Steve?"

Slight pause before, I wished the ground could have opened up and swallowed me, with the reply.

Sarah 2: "Oh it's OK, HE SLEPT WITH US!"

Angela: "Well I'm shocked, where is he?"

Sarah 1: "Oh he's sat right behind us!"

Now Angela could be a pretty foreboding person, so when she sat down next to me without a 'good morning' I realised an explanation (and it better be a good one) was needed!

"Well, Angela, it's like this, I returned late from the theatre…" and proceeded to explain the whole 'Peter O'Toole' saga by which time she was 'in awe' of my escapades, but her parting remark, before moving further down the coach, cut me to the quick! "I shall see that WE (meaning the rest of the staff) will need to keep our eye on you!"

It's a good job she didn't find out who had arranged the previous nights 'Pyjama Party!

I couldn't help but wonder if, the hotel room gods had got their revenge on my previous night's antics.

An unforgettable London trip, for me at least!

13 – WORLD WAR ONE REFLECTION

No time to breathe as *Bright Lights* beckoned and once again anticipation grew for our appearance on the Grand Theatre Stage.

The second-year contribution was a World War One tribute taking up a significant part of the second half of *Bright Lights.* It combined poetry, prose, singing and drama. This, if I say it myself, was a polished poignant and extremely effective piece.

I was tasked with researching and learning a 'letter home' to his wife from a Tommy (an ordinary soldier). Truth be told, I decided to 'make up' my contribution.

The letter was full of hope and anticipation as the soldier was due home on leave to see his wife and new born son.

He described vividly the conditions in which he found himself and how his close friend had been shot. Sadly, in my letter, as in the reality of 'The Great War' he was never to see his son, as he to, was 'killed in action' just before his leave was to commence.

His devoted wife was left heartbroken; she, along with her new born son, another casualty of war!

Yes, I had made it up, but as performed on the evening, along with all the other contributions it struck home with not just the cast but, with the audience, some of which, were moved to tears in this powerful presentation to which I was extremely proud to be part of.

I still have 'the note' that I wrote and no one, until now, was any the wiser, well maybe just a couple of people!

Both Angela Moran and Angela Hudson deserve immense credit in being able to get such mature performances out of such a young cast.

The piece, performed on Sunday 25th February 1990, ended with a song so powerfully delivered it sent shivers down your spine. I have seldom heard live, a song sung so poignantly. Louise R delivered the famous World War One song, 'Roses Are Blooming in Picardy'.

Wonderfully directed, staged and performed. A highlight of my time there!

I also took part in the stirring *Les Mis* finale, watched it the other day, someone waving a flag in my face throughout, quite right to, protecting the public from my mush!

We were once again so lucky to get the opportunity to perform *Bright Lights* at The Charter Theatre Preston on Sunday March 18th!

14 – FOUND 'FIND ME' AGAIN!

Find Me by now was taking shape. A short tour was arranged for various places including an open prison, schools and a nurse's home to perform in front of mental health staff.

One great thing amongst fellow drama students is that we support one another in whatever productions we were involved in.

Despite the 'heavy going' of *Find Me* and the nature of the production it was very well received when we previewed it in our theatre on March 2nd Emotionally draining, especially for the Verity's, but so rewarding to have performed such a mentally stimulating play.

We took the play on tour which lasted till the end of the summer term and our second year.

One venue early on I remember was one of the nurse's homes incorporated within Victoria Hospital. This created staging problems, as our performance and viewing area was no bigger than your ordinary front room!

Not sure how we managed, but perform it we did. Our audience was comprised of medical staff working within the mental health provision of the hospital.

Their life experience of actually confronting mental health was enlightening and helped us understand more the complexities of mental health. We had a Q&A afterwards, but was unsure as to who was asking the questions and who was answering them.

There were more tour dates scheduled for the summer term but, now the tour was 'put on hold' to allow the dreaded and 'nerve-racking' LAMDA exams, which I managed to sidestep, for the time being, more of which in a mo!

Back at college, the night before *Find Me*, the other second year group performed Willy Russell's *Blood Brothers*, the play, not the musical, both excellent.

In fact, I've been privileged over the years to see the musical, including in the West End, several times with at least three different Nolan Sisters playing the lead role.

15 – NO BANGING!

As performers, each group needed help to stage their play, setting the stage, bring on props and play in sound effects etc!

I was to be the other second year groups stage manager for *Blood Brothers.* A safe pair of hands you may think, as I was also ASM (work it out for yourself) in the forthcoming musical at the Grand, so what could possibly go wrong in having someone with my experience who really knows what they are doing!

Well, nothing in the dress rehearsal. In an inspired piece of casting, the two twin brothers in that group Jez C and Nick C, played Micky and Edward, the twins in the play.

I won't spoil the plot for those who haven't lived on planet Earth and haven't seen it but, the 'denouement' (had to check the spelling for that word!) hinged on gun being fired.

I think because the twins were extremely proficient in magic, they somehow managed to commandeer a pistol that fired blanks. I agreed that the sudden shock of a pistol being fired was much more realistic than a sound affect.

Everything had run smoothly, no gaffs on or off stage. The big moment had come, script in hand I raised the pistol aloft, on cue, pulled the trigger, NOTHING!

"Pull the bloody trigger," I could hear one of them mumble

I pulled it again… nothing. I cannot, as those who have seen it will testify, tell you how crucial split-second timing is for this. Even a second delay and the dramatic conclusion is lost.

In a now slightly agitated louder voice, which I'm sure some of the audience must have heard, "For f***'s sake pull the f***ing trigger." I did and this time it went off with such a loud bang that made the cast jump and the poor audience shot six feet in the air!

Not the dramatic ending we wanted, or the performers deserved. The cast took their bows, then recriminations started, for which I took full responsibility.

None of us found out why the starting pistol didn't go off when planned. I was truly sorry for ruining what was, up until then, a great performance. I can't be 100% sure, but I think I was forgiven. It's a wonder I wasn't shot with the damn thing!

16 – THERE WILL NOW BE A SHORT INTERMISSION

I mentioned about 'sidestepping' the LAMDA exams earlier. My 'night job' was (and still is) a DJ. I was fortunate back then to have an annual contract with a cruise ship. That year, I was made an offer I couldn't refuse.

Instead of a summer holiday, an opportunity had arisen to DJ on board the liner for a month's cruise over Easter '90, around the Caribbean! It was an opportunity too good to pass up despite being away from the place I just loved going to on a daily basis.

I know it's a 'no brainer' college or Caribbean Cruise? but, it wasn't that easy a decision, well alright then it was!

Although student holidays in term time were quite rightly frowned upon Brian, had earlier given his blessing and said I could sit the LAMDA exams in June, which I duly did.

What an adventure that was but, that's another story for another day and maybe, yet another book. Suffice to mention, it was a trip of a lifetime!

17 – I CAN'T BREATHE!

I loved my 'working holiday' but couldn't wait to get back to college where I found rehearsals for *The Pajama Game* in full swing.

So, I could feel that I was involved in the production, I offered my services backstage. As show time approached once again you could sense that nervous expectation at being given the opportunity to perform at one of the greatest theatres in the country!

We performed *The Pajama Game* at the Grand Theatre from 22nd-26th May 1990.

For those who have had that wonderful on-stage performance experience you will fully comprehend just what an adrenalin rush, in not just performing but, the acclaim of an audience can bring. Yes, a short term high, but for the inspiration it gave, ensured some would pursue a career in, at best 'an uncertain' but, glorious 'world of the Performing Arts'!

And so it was with all our students over many years, most of which were just beginning their careers. For some this week, the Grand Theatre stage would be the pinnacle of their 'big theatre experience'. For even if they diversified and took up another related, or unrelated, career paths, they would NEVER get this once, or maybe twice, in a lifetime opportunity! (Apart from Dean T and Gary Y, who may have reached double figures if you count *Bright Lights*!)

For others this was to be the start of an incredible life long journey, that once in your blood you just have to peruse.

In either of the above there is nothing like at that age, or any age for that matter, being given that opportunity that most grabbed with both hands.

Research has led me to believe that our students who, over many decades, had that opportunity that many aspiring performing arts students in other parts of the country didn't get, was along with The London Theatre visit, was THEE major contributing factor as to the success of the course and many of our students.

With Brian at the helm and the rest of the staff in support, it was no wonder back then, (in fact until the Grand experience finished in 1999 and The London Trip shortly afterwards) that, our students achieved MORE than the national average of success in stage, TV and film!

The Pajama Game would not have achieved such great heights without the above and beyond efforts of Brian, Angela's H&M, Jim, Debbie and Wendy. Added to this now was Alan Evans, who was a dab hand at set and stage design!

Opening night went well and we were set for a great run. The following day, we had a matinee and evening performance.

I had, during the matinee, a yummy bag of sweets (Lion's Sports Mixture's) which I foolishly left out for others to help themselves.

Feeling miffed that some students had 'nicked' them I decided during the interval between performances to visit my local joke shop for some special sweets. Whilst in the joke shop, I also purchased a little item that I thought may come in handy for later on in the week.

Back at the theatre I emptied several different types of joke sweets into my now empty sweet bag and once the evening show had started left them out.

I was happy to note that my bag of sweets was gradually being consumed. It was most amusing to stand backstage and watch numerous students, some of which had blue lips, and others more severe symptoms of having 'hot pepper syndrome', looking for any liquid they could lay their hands on to quench their thirst, some having to go on stage and perform, red of face and ready to explode!

The good thing from my prospective, until now, no one had any idea as to whose sweets, they had originally pilfered and more to the point, who had caused such backstage mayhem!

No apologies this time, although there is one coming up in a mo!

I'd also like to pay tribute to the student who diligently went round all the shoe shops asking for empty boxes. Not sure what use she thought they may be to our production of *The Pajama Game* but, seeing her stagger in the stage door just before the matinee ended piled high with shoe boxes was a tremendous effort. Well done and thank you, Denise G!

We had a great week at the Grand, including all the after-performance social gatherings.

Fiona M was a fantastic stage-manager. I really enjoyed my time working with her, a lovely person who, at that time, I struck up a great friendship with.

All good things must come to an end and all too quickly our run was also coming to its finale.

Not before an opportunity for a little 'on stage high jinx's'!

My problem, granted one of my own makings, is that once you gain a reputation for practical jokes you get blamed for ALL of them, something I found to my cost in, not just this production but, subsequent productions, fair do's!

Three practical jokes were played on that penultimate night, the Friday as I recall, two of which I take full responsibility for.

The two main leads were Sarah M (yes, one of the infamous Y-Fronts Sarah's) and the evergreen Gary Y (yes, he of the World Record Holder, for most student productions at the Grand).

Dave had a prominent part. In one scene, whilst delivering dialogue he went over to the cooler to pull out 'a cold one' which, as you've probably already guessed, had been vigorously shaken prior to it being placed in the fridge, for him to pull the ring, emptying the entire contents over him and the stage Not clever!

One of the most romantic songs in the show is 'Hey There'. Sarah M had to sing this whilst looking into a full-length mirror, which wasn't really a mirror at all but, gave the illusion as such to the audience.

Someone (not me) had placed on this full-length mirror, a blown up (if that's the right phrase) life size, male nude picture that only she could see!

Sarah M had to sing this heartfelt meaningful ballad whilst stood in front of it. What a pro, she never missed a beat! Exiting stage left to rapturous applause, she came straight over to me and without a word, I copped a slap across the mush! Even though I was 'not guilty' on this occasion, incrementally though, it was fully deserved!

The second act opens with the show's most memorable scene, Hernando's Hideaway!

We had the entire interval to set this dark secluded tavern. As many tables and chairs as we could cram on stage and all set with a toast of wine served in plastic stem glasses for ALL the cast to drink!

Obviously it wasn't real wine, but just the right colour of blackcurrant.

The scene, which was wonderfully choreographed, ended with the entire cast on stage raising a toast and knocking back the blackcurrant drink in one!

Exit the cast leaving Dave, who played the tavern drunk, to empty the dregs from each glass into his tankard, then for him to down it in one. Blackout, then curtain!

Any guesses? Who remembers my trip earlier in the week to the joke shop where a little item was purchased?

In my entire time at Performing Art's College, this was to be my 'PIECE DE RESISTANCE' of, on stage 'practical jokes.

The tiny bottle to which I speak, had skull and crossbones in red drawn on it! In all honesty I never realised how potent tabasco sauce was, but a drop in each vessel, proved to be, more than lethal.

Said moment arrived. Knocking back the toast, immediately you could see the look of fear in the cast eyes, as their faces looked like they were going to explode!

They were the lucky ones. Poor Dave had to stay on stage and complete his nightly ritual of emptying the dregs into his tankard, then downing it in one!

I can see his face to this day as he completed this, with the stage still 'live' turning 90 degrees to see me in the wings waving at him, whilst he (quite justifiably) mouthed, with his back to the audience, "YOU BASTARD!"

One poor girl, Jo Walsh, I felt sorry for, as she had a solo immediately after Hernando's Hideaway.

I saw her running around backstage saying "I can't breathe, I can't breathe, my mouths on fire!" Luckily, I had a bottle of water to hand, which she also downed in one, told me I was a saviour then, went on stage to sing as well as ever!

I do regret many of my 'on stage' pranks as they could ruin or compromise the production, but not that one. The cast, including Dave, took it in good 'spirits' looking back, still amusing, for me at least, but most unprofessional!

18 – THE AWARD GOES TO THE GIRL WITH THE 'BIGGEST ASSETS'

An after-show party was arranged at The West Coast. Ex-students, including John S and Craig K were there as well as the staff. The awards were, how can I put this, erm, un-PC, wrong and darn right offensive!

I won't bore you here with all the awards, just a couple.

Unknown to most. I wrote the awards, in other words, provided the ammunition for 'others' to fire. In turn I got various students including Dave, who should have known me better by then, to read out the nominations and winners.

Light blue touch paper and retire!

Dave read out nominations to a hushed room (not an easy ask) on a makeshift stage, 'The Girl with the Biggest Assets' award, He reads out a short list of girls with, the potential to make the big time along with, how can a put this delicately? I can't! (You get the picture) Actually, smut was never the intention, just a necessary by-product to arrive at the punchline!

After the shortlist was read, which brought a smugness and a large grin to the short-listed nominee's, Dave opened the envelope, read it to himself, turns to me and says, once again but this time audible,

"You bastard"

"The winner of the person with the biggest assets award goes to Wendy Schwarzkachel"!

That was to be the second time in as many nights Dave had cause to blacken my good name!

A little context before the next award: Jim had an excellent reputation in getting the best out of our voices, he even had a choir. Maliciously, I noted, at a college concert, that the majority of his female singing group just happened to be blonde! (Purely coincidence) I duly noted this for future reference!

Longevity student record holder, Dean T, I think presented this award

Nominees for the 'Jim Thomas Blond of Year Award' (at which point Dean released a ream of joined printed paper when unfolded reached the floor. suggesting lots of names) He read half a dozen, before naming, to rapturous cheers. Andrea K as the winner!

Now this might have been more amusing if Jim's wife had not have been in attendance, a point I failed to realize, I genuinely didn't know she was! Honest!

I'm not sure who was more embarrassed: me, Jim, his wife or Andrea, not Dean though!

Both Jim and Wendy and all the other 'dubious' winners took it in good spirits, although when Jim's wife found out who was responsible for the awards, she asked me if it were true that Jim only had blonde girls in his choir. I reassured her it wasn't and said "I sincerely hope I didn't get him in trouble", adding "I hope he doesn't have to sleep in the dog house tonight".

John S came up to me after the awards. We had a short chat, he said he'd "enjoyed the awards" adding "I was really cool". Praise indeed for one who is the epitome of that word!

I felt somehow that night, those 'near the knuckle' awards, that I was now 'accepted' as 'one of the lads' something upon till then, I felt only on the fringes of.

19 – FAREWELL, BOSOM BUDDY

Summer term at college was usually a bit of a wind down. We did have our *Find Me* tour to complete which sadly finished on a bit of a whimper. Some of the group had left, which meant adjustments to the cast.

It ended early one evening outside Highfield School. Alan Evans informing us that our scheduled performance was cancelled! That day coincided with the last day of our second year and most of the remaining group were leaving.

My 'bosom buddy' Dave had secured a place at the prestigious Drama Centre, others also were off to pastures new.

So, sat on a wall outside the school with no mobile phones to take one another's future unknown landline numbers, we all said our goodbyes. I never saw some of them again!

Others, like Dave, I stayed in touch with and despite that anti-climatical end to term, none of us could deny that the last two years had been a great adventure. We not only learnt a lot but, LOVED AND ENJOYED doing it!

One final postscript for my second year was the LAMDA exam I missed in March. I'm pleased to say that I, along with then a third year, Sam K, attended the Imperial Hotel, Blackpool on the 22nd June 1990 and passed this time with CREDIT thus, ending on a high, my second year on the Foundation Drama Course!

I also graduated with flying colours on the more academic City and Guild's Journalism Course. I can't thank Kaye Keir enough for the help and support and was also proud of myself as academically, at school, my grades were poor

I can categorically state that, over those two wonderful years, I owed much to Brian Hindle who was inspirational in not just mine, but my fellow student's development in acting and performance skills.

The culmination of the course was normally two years but as I've mentioned, there was an opportunity for some to return for a third year. There could be various reasons for this, Dean T would be a good person to ask as, he seemed to be the 'perennial student'.

One thing for sure, due to arrival of Alan Evans, DRAMATIC course changes were a-foot.

I too was at a crossroads. Were my student days over?

20 FANCY, ME A TEACHER!

The next academic year back in September 1990 saw a new two-year BTEC National Diploma start.

On successful completion this would enable students, should they so wish, to progress to university. This more 'vocational' route was much better suited to the skills of most 'performers'

Entry level from school was five GCSEs at C Grade or above, or a one-year completion of the existing Drama Foundation course for those without them!

There were some who wanted to complete their second year foundation course.

In returning for a third year, I was extremely fortunate to be offered by Kaye Keir a part-time teaching post on the journalism course that I had only just graduated from in the last academic year.

I say fortunate because although there was a teaching vacancy and I had passed the course with flying colours, I had no previous teaching experience. Sometimes in life just being in the right place at the right time helps.

What I set about doing straight away was to, establish a mutually beneficial link between the Journalism Course and Performing Arts.

That link also helped me land more valuable teaching experience in Performing Arts, especially in promoting the department!

21 - AND STILL A STUDENT

As my teaching was only part-time, I still was able to carry on my student duties and joined in with what was to be the final second year of the foundation course. Most of last year's first years and other more mature students like Katy N and of course Dean T, started on the ND course but there were still enough students for a small second year rabble that I was fortunately able to dip in and out of.

Brian continued to be the driving light of the course. I can honestly say that, in his weekly lessons we had with him, even Shakespeare, which I initially loathed, I came away with, a sense of achievement..

Quality theatre education, combined with the actual enjoyment of the process which, he managed to deliver appropriately to all levels, from basic training, adult day classes and right the way through to university level made him, for me a unique human being the likes of which unfortunately, are few and far between these days. I can count on the fingers of one hand the people in my life who have made that difference and had such an influence.

Unsurpassed, for all who entered his domain, (usually room 028) This partly explains just How Cool Brian was!

Throughout my third year, Brian continued to be my mentor. Firstly, as a student then with his expertise as a tutor in, explaining 'gently and kindly' to me, how I was to make the transformation from student to staff member.

My recollections of my third year as a student are few and far between however, I do remember fairly early on in the term, when after the staff have assessed the strength of our new intake, what musical is to be performed at The Grand the following Spring, Spring, Spring!

This year it was to be *Seven Brides for Seven Brothers*. (For those unaware the above repeated word is a song title from that production!)

Slight problem (one of which I address later in the Christmas Review!): can we muster seven brothers?

Now where there was a deficit of 'the males of the species' it more than made up for by those with the 'alternative plumbing'! In fact, they could have cast the brides twice over, which is exactly what they did, cast fourteen brides!

Because of the shortage of men, guess who was seconded into the production? Yes, little old me!

Jim's immortal flattering remark to me, maybe similar in encouraging Dave to be in Pyjama Game!

"Steve, there's a lovely part which I'd like you to audition for."

"Oh yes," I replied, "Which part is that?"

"Mr Perkins," said Jim. "Don't worry though, you won't have to sing!"

One of the better back-handed compliments I've had!

I decided to 'av a bash' nothing to lose and great to be in a production. It only took me three years to pluck up the courage!

Unfortunately, auditions included a song. Oh dear!

Jim and I came up with a suitable song, which I learnt

I performed it better than I thought I was capable of. Then again, not much could go wrong with 'Rhythm of The Rain' Could it?

One of the things I do remember in that first term that year, was receiving a letter which I still treasure, from Dave Royle saying "How's it going? Mr Bradshaw, teacher, give them shit!" "You have come a long way since 1988" My reply back, we both had!

He went on to say about how he was "settling well on the course" and "what an eye-opener it was". "In order at having no inhibitions with all fellow students in the first week we had to 'get naked' on stage, as well as having to share changing facilities." (lucky swine!)

Good thing that never happened at college in the first week. I'd have run a mile!

We exchanged letters a few times in that first year and I just knew, not just from what he wrote but, from what I saw him achieve at college and through his own self-determination and natural talent, he would make it.

He most definitely did 'make it' and I loved watching his performances over the years, especially as Sergeant Wield in *Dalziel and Pascoe*, still to this day when repeated on TV.

A couple of years ago, whilst at my second home (the Grand Theatre) I bumped into Colin Buchanan (Pascoe) who was performing in a play. We met afterwards. He paid a great compliment to Dave saying "What a great actor he was" and "How much he had enjoyed working with him".

He did say that Warren Clarke (Dalziel) wanted Dave to stay in the series but Dave had wanted to move on!

Miss you lots, Dave. Thanks for the memories!

22- THE NEXT ITEM!

Doesn't time go fast when you are enjoying yourself, already it was Christmas Review time!

I was able that year to direct the review but, to ensure I wouldn't be blamed for everything (after all I did have my reputation to consider now, I was a member of the academic staff!) I persuaded Liz H and Sue D to help audition, produce and stage what was for me, to be my favourite and final Review!

The whole programme was spot on. Some great act's including Bert and Ernie, (Steve C, Benji N and Tony F)

The Connie Sisters (Jez, Tony, Benji and Steve C)

and Caroline who nailed The Greatest Love of All!

I also set up a member of the academic staff which, I was now part of. It worked a treat!

Although the idea was mine, Debra Smythe should take the credit for the successful choreography.

I had struck up a repour with several of the academic staff one of which, Tim Davis was an excellent sport and had a great sense of humour. He would need it!

The Morris dance involved initially four girls – Fiona, Caroline, Donna and Jane – who came on in Morris dance costume, complete with sticks that they all clicked together at the appropriate spot in the dance.

Fiona then interrupted the routine saying "Stop, stop, this is boring. What we need are some men!"

Now at this point I need to inform you that I, along with Mark D, Bradley M and one other male along with the aforementioned girls, had secretly rehearsed and choreographed this wonderful Morris dance, with the copious and obligatory much 'clicking of sticks' in the middle!

So, when the girls came into the audience 'looking for men', Mark, Bradley and I were well and truly rehearsed plant's!

The fourth one I asked them to choose from the audience, which went down a storm with the academic students and staff who were watching was, yes, you've guessed it, poor Tim, who didn't have a clue he had been set up. As he commented to me en-route to the stage, "Oh they've got you up as well have they!"

Once on stage we were asked to 'roll up our trousers' and given a clicking stick each. Cue music, off we go.

So, there we were, seven of us who'd rehearsed this dance and Tim looking bewildered, trying to make sense of what was happening.

He couldn't work out how we seemed to grasp the routine. Worse was to come. We had eight long clicking sticks which we clicked together, when we came into the centre. Unfortunately for Tim, his clicking stick was made out of balsawood and every time all eight of us centred and clicked, a bit of his broke off! By the end of the routine, he was left holding a piece no bigger than his finger!

His poor vacant gaze, into the audience said it all!

You can imagine the reaction he got from the audience, some of which were his own students, who also had no idea it was a set up!

When we talked afterwards, he congratulated me on my Morris dancing ability. I suppose that was the ideal opportunity to confess, but I didn't. It was sometime later he found out and Tim, being the man he is, took it in great spirit!

There was to be one last hoorah before I retired from being directly involved in the Christmas Review, although I was for many years to come, asked to 'vet the content of each subsequent one' because of this very sketch, which one or two staff may have thought, went too far!

I wrote and directed it, but deliberately distanced myself from being in it to let others take the blame!

The Next Item!

Another 'light blue touch paper and retire' occasion!

With the benefit of hindsight, especially as I was unaware at the time that I would shortly become a member of the Performing Art's staff, I wouldn't have dared written it!

I am still unclear even now, all these years later, how the staff were unaware I had written that sketch, however, back then, apart from 'sleepover incident' I had, quite naturally, somewhat of an unblemished reputation, which I worked hard at maintaining, especially with the staff!

Looking at it from the staff's point of view, as I once had to many years later, I can see now, that exaggerating characteristics of such lovely people would, in a packed theatre, full of over exuberant student's cause much cringworthiness and embarrassment to them, which wasn't my intention. I saw it as just a little 'light hearted' end of term fun.

So here for the first time, looking back at the original script, is how '*The Next Item*' stetch came to life.

First of all I listed the college staff and what their individual personality traits were and then exaggerated them to the extent of 'lampooning them'.

Dean K did a brilliant Jim, his wah wah wah wah's, went down a storm, as did Cher's OTT Angela Moran. Darren M played Brian and Jo A, took the part of Angela Hudson.

Costume was crucial.

Jim – (Dean K) jacket and white shirt big grin.

Angela Moran – (Cher) Black dress, big black sun glasses.

Brian – (Darren W) Mustard yellow jumper, not sure why Darren wore a flat cap!?

Angela – (Jo A) Fluffy lamb's wool cardigan and because of her softly spoken tone of delivery, a megaphone in which to speak her lines through.

Obviously, it's much better seen than described, however the main thrust of the piece was just to have a bit of fun, admittedly at the staff's expense!

There was a split stage, where the action developed in two 'freeze-framed' scenarios.

On one half of the stage, students wondering what musical would be chosen at the staff's high level 'liquid lunch' meeting at The Grand Hotel (behind the college)

Students, being students, were suggesting to one another, a modern, up-to-date musical should be chosen, preferably something they have heard of but, realising its more likely to be something they've never heard of like previous productions of *The Boyfriend* or *The Pajama Game*!

The other half of the stage showed the staff, chaired by Brian, sat round discussing what musical to do that year.

A little flavour of how it went:

Scene – Lunchtime at The Grand Hotel, waitress (Julie M) waits to take order!

Brian – Waitress, our usual please.

Angela H – (softly spoken) I thought we might do.

(The rest straining to hear)

Brian – (interrupting her) Project, dear, project!

Waitress returns with drinks order including, a bottle of gin for Angela Moran

Brian – Could we have a side order of a megaphone, please!

Jim – I thought we could do something with BIG, BIG PRODUCTION NUMBERS (waving his hands in the air), lots of great songs, *Chicago* or *Cabaret.*

Brian – Are they not a little 'risqué' for our students?

Jim – Think of Wendy, no elaborate costumes to make, just the bare minimum underwear, I can picture it now! (He laughs as only Jim can. Wah wah wah.)

Angela Moran – (swigging from bottle) Oh no, we can't do something students would like, I've decided it's either *The Wiz* or *South Pacific*.

Brian – But the students won't know those.

Angela Moran – Exactly!

(Waitress returns with megaphone)

Angela Moran – Waitress, another bottle of gin, please!

Brian – (handing Angela Hudson the megaphone) Sorry, Angela, you were saying…

Angela Hudson – (speaking now, through the megaphone) Something like *Hair* could pull the crowds in!

Jim – Is that the one where the cast are naked and the plots a bit thin? Yes and a bonus for Wendy. It will mean less costuming for her! Yes, I'm all for that! (wah wah wah!)

Angela – (confused) Oh, I don't know now!

Brian – No, no. we have our reputation to think of.

Jim – Pity!

The waitress returns with yet another bottle of gin for Angela Moran.

Angela Moran – (to waitress) What's your favourite musical?

Waitress – (thinks for a mo) I don't know (then randomly declares) *Seven Brides for Seven Brothers*.

Staff look at each other then, simultaneously and declare BINGO!

(Blackout)

Cut to 45 minutes later, staff fast asleep, gin bottles piled high, Waitress wakes them,

Waitress – Come on, you lot, you'll be late back. They won't let you in your lesson if you're more than ten minutes late!

(There was a rule back then if students were more than ten minutes late, they weren't allowed in the lessons)

Meanwhile, back at college the students eagerly await the return of the staff from their crucial high level secret lunchtime meeting to determine that year's musical!

Girl 1 – I wonder what the musical is going to be this year?

Girl 2 – I hope it's something we like *Chicago* or *Cabaret* maybe?

Girl 1 – You're joking, we never do anything we like (reference to the two previous musicals). It's more likely to be ones we've never heard of like *The Wiz* or *South Pacific*!

Girl 2 – Ah here they are now, back from their 'business meeting'

The staff return from their 'working lunch'

Jim – Well it's been a long agonising decision, but we think we've come up with a winner!

Angela Moran – (staggers forward) Are you ready for this… Seven Brides for Seven Brothers!

Much hooping and a hollowing and 'high fives' from the assembled students glad, at last, the staff who deliberated long and hard have chosen wisely!

Cue narrator Bradley M

Bradley – The Drama department suffers from a major problem, BOYS, or, should I say, the lack of them. The ratio of girls to boys is about 7 to 1, which creates headaches when casting. However, we can now proudly present the World Premier of *Fourteen Brides for Three and a Half Brothers*, with a bit of luck it might be four if Mark grows a bit before the show!

(That last remark was one of the few I regret, albeit he did get a lot of sympathetic 'ahhs' from the girls in the audience at the time but, it was a cheap shot at how tall Mark was at the time, for which I once again apologise for!)

Cue - Much 'on stage' mayhem ensued as, how fourteen brides copped off with three and a half brothers. The other brothers were played by Jim's music stands with cardboard cut-outs of brothers, attached for the girls to dance round the stage with!

The scene culminated in a wedding service conducted by 'the preacher' (Dean K) facing the audience in his 'religious garbs' only to reveal, when turning round with his back to the audience and to face the brides and brothers, 'frilly knickers and stocking and suspenders' which, as you can imagine, ended the sketch in uproar!

I have not taken as much personal satisfaction as I did in writing, devising, casting, directing and staging *The Next Item* and the cast exceeded my expectations!

I think the staff took it in good spirits, although Angela Hudson confessed many years later that she never wore a lamb's wool cardi to college ever again!

After The Christmas Review antics continued when, the student population descended on The Tavern for our end of term Christmas drink.

I was unable to partake in the much drinking as, an hour later I was expected back at college for the entire staff (academic and drama) Christmas party and it wouldn't have looked good turning up at the end of my first term as tutor 'worse for wear', so just had a soft drink!

I still had with me the megaphone used by Jo A in portraying Angela Hudson in the Christmas Review. Shame not to make further use of it in this crowded student venue!

Cue megaphone – "A message for Sarah M, can she please phone the STI clinic, your results are now in!"

Much raucous laughter in the pub ensued, and as you can imagine. Sarah M was not best pleased, grabbing the megaphone from me before I was asked to leave by the proprietor!

Fancy, a college tutor being thrown out of a pub! I needed to be on way anyway! Back to college for a nice sedate 'Jacob's join'.

Having just been thrown out of the pub and the instigator of the 'near the knuckle' Christmas revue, it was therefore most ironic if not a little embarrassing, when back at college, I received a glowing report on my first term as a tutor.

Talk about being given a break! Three weeks, for Christmas and New Year!

OUR GRAND THEATRE
PRODUCTIONS (1986-1999)

Calamity Jane, 1986

Guys & Dolls, 1987

West Side Story, 1988

The Boyfriend, 1989

The Pajama Game, 1990

7 Brides for 7 Brothers, 1991

The New Pirates of Penzance,
1992

Kiss Me Kate, 1993

Fiddler on the Roof, 1994

Guys & Dolls, 1995

Chicago, 1996

Twelfth Night, 1996

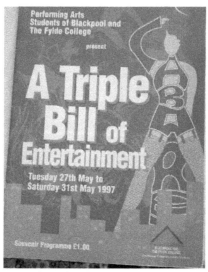

A triple Bill of Entertainment, 1997
Performed at the Pavilion Horseshoe
Theatre, within The Winter Gardens
complex (Cabaret – Alice in Wonderland –
Westenders)

Hot Mikado, 1998

A Midsummer Night's
Dream, 1998

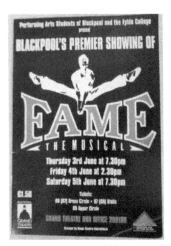

Fame, 1999

The Lion, the Witch and the
Wardrobe, 1999

The Facebook group, HOW COOL WAS BRIAN HINDLE (created by Lorraine Hodgson) has 100's of pictures and comments from ex-students of all era's. Well worth a delve into if you don't get out much!

23 – 'I DON'T BELIEVE IT'

A new year was heralded by our annual London trip. This year to The Regent's Palace Hotel, Piccadilly Circus, right in the heart of London, as there was 'no room at the inn' for us at our usual haunt, The Royal National in Russell Square.

My third London visit was somewhat of an eye-opener. No more 'freedom of the city'!

As I was now on the staff, some silly person thought it may be a good idea for the Journalism students to 'make up the number's'. (I should have kept my trap shut!)

Kaye Keir and I arranged a much 'tighter' schedule of visits including, a visit to Capitol Radio and watching the recording of a new sit-com.

Here's one for the ole timers, *One Foot in the Grave*.

Yes, interesting to see how television works, but, the mechanics of it, the 'stop start' approach when the director kept shouting "CUT" every few minutes, added to which the programme was shot out of sync, left the live audience bereft of laughter.

For me the worst bit of recorded programmes (and some live ones), is a floor manager holding a sign up saying 'laugh now'!

As I grow older, I realise I have a 'touch of the Victor Meldrew' in me. I cannot watch or stand 'canned or recorded' laughter!

I think that evening I took the journalists to see a proper production, *Blood Brothers* a sure-fire winner, even for budding journalists!

The following day it was to Capitol Radio. It was then the most listened to commercial station. We had an informative insight into commercial radio. Little did I know then that before too long I also would achieve my life-long ambition, to be a DJ on the radio. That 28 year dream job and all it entailed is another story but for now I was about to see my radio hero, Kenny Everett! Another up-and-coming presenter, Steve

Penk, showed us the ropes and gave myself and the students a flavour of what it was like in speaking to millions of people who were hanging on his every word! The students loved the visit as did I.

In a strange twist of fate a few years later, Steve worked with my friend and colleague Jon Culshaw, Jon, back then was. the voice of many a wind-up phone calls including one as William Hague to the then Prime Minister Tony Blair, all good fun!

The age of the mobile phones had not long dawned, both Kaye and I had the latest technology, a 'A Nokia brick!

Later that day, whilst we all had a little free time, I received a call off Kaye that, one of the students had been run over!

Although, after a visit to the local A&E and with no visible or underlying injuries, Kaye thought it best to return home on the train with the girl, not only for the student's own 'well-being' but to 'reassure' concerned parents, that although obviously worrying, it was in fact only a minor accident.

Glad to say there were no further incidents to report.

In fact, looking back on most of our London trips, many of which I ended up arranging, apart from the odd naughty student being sent home, we had very few calamities. I always found it best to, try and return with the same number of students one sets out with, avoids complications back home. Can be a tad frustrating for a parent collecting their off-spring to find out that not so little Johnny isn't on the coach!

24 – THE NORTHERN BRIGHT LIGHTS

Returning to college from London, could I suppose, be a bit of an anti-climax but as so often was the case, no time to reflect as *Bright Lights* was soon to be upon us.

On Sunday 24th Feb '91 we were back home at the Grand Theatre, some excellent pieces, including an excerpt from our musical *Seven Brides for Seven Brothers*.

The main thrust seemed to be a big second half tribute to Broadway, which for some reason a dance number called 'Let's Go Crazy' stands out!

Once again there was to be a further bash at the Charter Theatre Preston for *Bright Lights*.

Back at college, Brian's LAMDA exams for the remaining Foundation students gave everyone a focus. Not for me though. I had my own *Bright Lights* show to prepare for. It was to be for me, the Aurora Borealis, The Northern Lights!

My annual jaunt on board the cruise ship awaited! What a sight. Not quite the sight to behold as the sight of sixty 'odd' students in dungarees but it came mighty close!

25 - YEKATERINBURG

On my return rehearsals for our groups play commenced.

The Anastasia File by Royce Ryton was most definitely Brian's conception; he knew the difficulties the production would embrace and by the time we had watched the film *Anastasia* and read through the play, SO DID WE!

The play centres around the massacre of the entire Romanov Russian Royal Family at Yekaterinburg (I'm thankful once again for spell check!) in July 1918.

Several years after the massacre, later in the play, one of the children, now a young adult, turns up in America purporting to be Anastasia who had supposedly been killed along with her family!

The play was extremely complex. The amount of research that went into, not just the play but, the credibility of the girls claims to be Anastasia, for me turned this production into an investigation in trying to ascertain the facts behind her claim! Added to this, not just the learning of the play, which was set in two different time zones and countries but, the delivery of the lines proved a hard ask.

Anyone ever tried to do a credible Russian accent? No neither had I till then and I'm not sure back then, I ever mastered it!

The cast as I remember it were:

Cher W, who played an extremely convincing Anastasia and without a doubt, was the stand-out performer in this production.

I am sure there was a larger cast but I can only remember Andrea K, Sue D, then Bradley M and I playing numerous male characters.

However, 'The learning of line's' and the performances of this production would have to wait till after our annual Grand Theatre production which, was getting ever nearer!

26 – FOURTEEN BRIDES FOR SEVEN BROTHERS

Now as you recall from the Christmas Review my skit on *Seven Brides for Seven Brothers* (*Fourteen Brides for Three and a Half Brothers*) became half right.

There were to be two sets of Brides, Team A and Team B, alternating, with three performances each. Karen R (who was also lead in *The Boyfriend*) and Caroline S were the female leads with Tony F and Mark R the male leads.

Angela Hudson did a great job in directing and how Debbie managed to choregraph this, especially with my two left feet, is still a miracle of modern-day science!

Part of the overall success of our college productions over many years has been Jim's ability to hire the best local musicians. Year after year the students have been so lucky to work with an orchestra befitting a professional production and this year was to be no exception!

The college, five years earlier had done *Calamity Jane* so Wendy's costuming was, for once a little less stressful than normal. Wendy also had a cute dog which, she had trained for the camp fire 'do-si-do' scene, surely to good an opportunity to miss! more of which in a mo!

Dress rehearsal had not gone well at all, but there's a saying for those who are involved in productions: bad dress, good performance!

The good performance that resulted on our opening night, (Tues 21–25th May 1991) was more down to Angela's and Debbie's notes.

Don't underestimate Angela's quiet persona, she has a great ability of getting the best out of performers as a director and it turned out to be an excellent production.

Although my character had several scenes, I was not always on stage, which enabled me to get up to my 'old tricks'.

It was not fair; I was blamed for all the high jinks that went on during the run.

There is a scene in which stew was served out of a cauldron, so when ladling onto the plates, as well as the stew (and much to the surprise of Caroline S) condoms were visibly seen being ladled out. It was NOT me (honest!).

What was me in this production, although not all on the same night, thankfully was:

- Locking G in the dressing room and despite much banging on the door to "let me out let me out" the poor girl missed her stage call!

- In the opening scene a 'promenade' of people including me as Mr Perkins and Tracie M as Mrs Perkins took place One night I swapped Mrs Perkins for a random girl and promenaded with her (Julie M). instead. Mrs Perkins caught us hand in hand and I 'got what for' off her. This shocking bit of upstaging of an 'on stage domestic' unfortunately took the audiences focus off the main front of stage dialogue. Reprehensible!

- Worse was to come, Mr and Mrs Perkins (myself and Tracie) had to kneel before the preacher, (tall Bradley M) who was facing the audience. Whilst in our kneeling positions, with our backs to the audience and level with his 'nethers' he was in full flow delivering his prayer to us, for the safe return of our daughter, I inadvertently blurted out, "Whilst you're down there!"

  Now I blame Tracie for not being able to contain her involuntary shoulder movements, which left the audience, but more to the point, our director Angela, in no doubt whatsoever that she was not in control, unforgivingly, copsing on stage! Quite rightly she was given a bollocking for being 'unprofessional'. Shameful behaviour, Mrs P!

- As I mentioned earlier, Wendy's well-trained dog played a part to in the production. Much too good an opportunity to waste! My favourite joke shop beckoned once more, this time, as I think you've guessed, for a nice fake (but extremely realistic) 'doggie doo'.

I helped set the scene for the 'camp fire dance' (brides and grooms stood in opposite lines and then collectively with their respective partners, in a wonderful choreographed piece, moved up and down in a perfect straight line, (well up till that night at least).

After setting the stage with the 'extra item' strategically placed I dashed up to the upper circle to view! Instead of the straight line that night, a 'semi-circle' was observed from above as, all the cast members looked to avoid treading in the 'doggie doo'. Having viewed this wonderful spectacle from above, I quickly dashed back down to the side of the stage where I was greeted by a Grand Theatre stagehand who turned to me with brush and shovel in hand and said "Never work with children and animals" and then Wendy in her own inevitable style, replying "My dog wouldn't do anything like that". Most unfair on me as I was trying to keep a straight face!

Fond memories of the production, I still refer to Tracie as 'Mrs P' when, from time to time, we exchange insults.

At the after-show party, I also collected the award for 'most milked line' "Sounds like old tabby has the croup." It was well-deserved and a horrendous piece of OTT acting!

27 AN OUTSTANDING PERFORMANCE

Back after the May Bank Holiday my two main tasks were ensuring completion of journalist's coursework and learning lines for The Anastasia File.

I had also missed my Gold Medal LAMDA. With Brian's guidance, I felt confident at performing these pieces to the best of my ability but it was not my main focus and for some reason, I can't even remember if I did, complete my Gold Medal.

No, my main focus was not letting our group down in this 'challenging' play that was proving the most difficult task of my 'student days'!

College was always quieter in the summer term as courses, especially academic ones, wound down.

Unfortunately, Kaye and I had a lot of chasing to do to ensure an 85% success rate for the course, which was required to enable it to run next year. Pleased to say, by the skin of our teeth, we did it!

Back in Performing Arts there was also another big 'in house production' *Stags and Hens*, performed at the college on June 12th 1991!

The students excelled in this Willy Russell play and it would be unfair of me to 'single out' one particular student, however I am going to!

The phrase 'single out' was indeed apt! All was going swimmingly when, all of a sudden there was a, how can I put this delicately, let's say, 'a wardrobe malfunction' with one of the female students (see 'single out' comment above). Modesty forbids me to name her in full, although our paths had crossed previously in 'The London Bedroom Scandal'.

There was much 'tittering' in the audience, but when 'all was safely gathered in' the action continued.

That evening I wrote a review, printed it out and, arriving early next morning, placed it on the notice board!

I wish I had saved a copy, even if it were only for the purposes of this book! It read something like:

Keeping abreast of an 'outstanding performance' by Sarah M, whose 'enormous potential was displayed to the full last night, showing off her considerable attributes to an appreciative audience, with such 'dramatic effect'.

I knew, for once there would be more interest than usual, at the student notice board but, even I was 'taken a-back' at the sheer volume of students who crowded round. At one point Alan Evans (not best pleased) dispersed them all.

The cast, who were in the production didn't arrive at college till later, so you can imagine how many had read it before action was taken by annon to remove said notice and seeking me out gave me a right ear full!

Poor girl, not just the megaphone incident after the Christmas Review and having to sing to a 'full length' nude male poster, on stage at The Grand Theatre in *The Pajama Game* not to mention along with her friend, being exposed to the dreaded Y-Fronts incident at The Royal National, now suffering indignation and humiliation because of 'a boob' during her stand out performance on the previous night!

We have had lots of talented performers over many years at college. Sarah M was not only one of them but a good sport to boot! (Once again, sorry.)

28 – BRIAN'S TOUR DE FORCE

I have to say I was dreading our college performance of *The Anastasia Files*, not only could I not master the different accents required in various roles I played but, to think it would be judged by my peers, left me with a sense of foreboding!

The play was performed at college right at the end of term on the 19th and 20th June 1991.

Not only a difficult play to perform but, especially for students, a very difficult one to watch!

We did our best, it was well received (as college productions usually are, supporting one another!) and I can say, as a person, I am now much more informed about the Russian Revolution and the Romanov Royal Family. Should the subject ever arise in 'day-to-day' conversation which, to date I'm happy to report it has not, I would be able to quote chapter and verse!

The one main thrust of the play was the authenticity of the girl purporting to be Anastasia. The play, when written, didn't finalise evidence one way or another but, history through new DNA techniques, was quickly evolving.

Through this, many years later in 2007, it was determined once and for all that... Well, I'll leave the mystery there for you to solve!

It was most appropriate however, that my college performance days ended as they began, (with a court case) shrouded in mystery!

Brian loved everything about this production, especially the research behind it, so a fitting tribute to him, that the cast ended the term and year performing this!

It was to be the end of my halcyon 'playing days', for which I owe the wonderful staff, especially Brian, a great debt of gratitude!

29 – THE END OF MY PLAYING DAYS (mostly)

Sorry as I was to leave my student days behind me, I was delighted to be offered by the Head of Department, Alan Evans, a 'staff position' the role of Marketing and Publicity for Performing Arts.

Wow, little ole me on the staff, thrilled and delighted to work with such loving and caring people. One thing slightly bothered me: would my 'practical jokes' have to be curtailed?

30 – THE ART OF TEACHING, OR IN MY CASE, THE ART OF ACTING WHILST TEACHING!

I have found in life, especially now I've experienced too much of it, that SINCERITY IS EVERYTHING! Once you have learnt to fake that, you've cracked it!

So as a new academic year dawned in September 1991, I joined the staff of the Performing Arts Department.

When I first joined the staff, without exception, they all made me feel most welcome.

Over the years we grew even closer. I remember having summer days out and overnight stays in Wendy's and Angela's caravans. Not only were we a close knit staff but we socialised, having meals out and theatre visits together!

I have never worked with, before or since such lovely, generous and kind-hearted people, as I did with Brian, Jim, Angela H, Debbie, Wendy, Angela M and Alan

We were more like 'family' than work colleagues, even our Head of Department Alan Evans became 'one of the family' a great testament to him excepting us all so readily.

This was to prove mutually beneficial. Alan knew that, if cover was needed for whatever reason one of us would be only too willing to jump in at short notice and cover subjects we didn't normally teach and he would make allowances for our occasional absences. I say occasional as, we all enjoyed not just working there but, one another's company. An absolute joy to go there, and along with, in the main, fantastic bunch of students who, for some, this was the first time in their lives that they were engaged and enjoying education and being with other 'liked minded' students and staff!

At first, my duties were 'Marketing and Promoting' the department, but pretty soon I ended up 'blagging it' in front of, mainly 'gullible students'. My acting skills would have to be put to good use. Not on the stage but, if front of the very students who were training to be actors!

I had no 'formal teaching qualifications', so for this, I at least needed to 'act' as though I knew what I was talking about!

The BTEC course was now in full swing and one of the core subjects was Arts Administration. Sounds a tad boring and to most performing arts students, whose skills and talents are more practical, IT WAS!

Without passing it though, students couldn't progress!

Creating your own CV, promoting, marketing and budgeting for productions were all 'the boring bits' performers weren't keen on!

Alan was great and gave me a helping hand. He had previously taught the unit, so in those early days I very much relied on him.

Once up and running, I did gain in confidence and the classroom became my 'performance space and stage'.

Some of my best ever performances in acting were to be in the classroom, acting as a strict tutor, in front of 'naïve first years' if I say so myself, I deserved an Oscar!

I kept this 'good guy, bad guy' image right up till when I left at the end of 2001. What a performer!

At college my 'persona' was a strict disciplinarian, most difficult to keep a straight face sometimes, especially when the second-year students, who knew what I was like and couldn't work out why the first years thought I was strict.

I had to be strict, it was the height of clubbing in Blackpool. Thursday night was seemingly 'mandatory club night' and my boring mandatory Arts Admin lesson was, guess when? Yes, first thing at 9.15 Friday morning!

Jim had given me a 'heads-up' by saying that the start of every lesson was like the curtain raising on a performance. If you're late, you've missed it!

A few weeks in and dwindling Friday morning numbers I threatened to come and take the register at the night club they all frequented. To everyone's surprise, a couple of weeks later I did.

Well, what an eye opener. You learn something new every day. It certainly taught me a lesson! Never again those shots they gave me were lethal but, as 'unwell' as I was, the next morning. I made it to class on time, asking the students politely if they wouldn't mind keeping their voices down!

31 – ALAN'S MAJOR BRAIN WAVE

Glad to say under Alan's regime, college rituals were maintained. First up was to choose the following May's musical production.

For the first time, now as a staff member I was involved in the decision making of what show to go for. I must admit holding back on choices as I felt their superior knowledge and judgement was paramount.

The only thing I needed to ensure from my perspective was, would the final choice of production put bums on seats as rising production costs would need to offset with box office receipts

Over the years, from the inception of The Grand Theatre shows the staff made some excellent choices of shows to fit not just the students' abilities but incorporating, year on year the growing numbers to the course, which was now proving problematical as last years production had shown having to double cast seven brides!

One of the foundation stones and ultimately successes of the course has been the annual musical. Still to this day whenever I talk to ex-students, its usually our annual show or *Bright Lights* productions they remember.

I think many would agree that *West Side Story* was probably the best but, close behind came productions like, *Guys and Dolls*, (twice) *Chicago* and Alan's inspired choice *The New Pirates of Penzance*, which turned out to be, for me, in my time there, the best production I was involved in.

As far as the staff were concerned, initially this was a 'left field' suggestion, maybe because I don't think to many of us had heard of it.

I knew the original which, would have been a difficult ask as Gilbert & Sullivan had become outdated as it was written over a hundred years ago in a style that the staff, (with the exception of the mercurial Jim Thomas) never mind the students, may find hard to comprehend! Not only that but, who would want to come and see it?

Alan did leave the choice of the production up to the staff who, would have to cast, rehearse and perform it and the bold decision was made, let's go for it!

This new version even included the famous 'Major General Rap' brilliantly delivered by Dean K!

Yes, Alan had picked a winner here alright, not only with various strands to the cast (pirates, policemen and daughters) there was also ample opportunity for the entire growing Performing Art's course to be involved!

My inspirational brain-wave was handing over the 'bums on seats' bit to the cast, who surely wouldn't want to perform to a half empty theatre. Eighty plus students could get their families and friends to come which, would account for a proportion of the box office. Added to that BTEC marks could be awarded for initiative in promoting the production. The more seats sold through these initiatives, the higher their final grade, would be in the marketing unit of the production!

Although we were still in the first term, casting for the show early meant rehearsals could commence on Wednesday afternoons, along with the *Bright Lights* production.

I'll speak more about the superb cast and crew at 'show time' just to mention that, in casting Dean K in the role of the Major General along with, the strength of the entire cast including chorus, we knew we had a 'sure fire' winning production'.

We had the makings of a 'standout production' but before then there was the little matter of the Christmas shindig.

For the first time in four years I wasn't involved in the production or performance of it. I was asked 'to 'vet' the acts, after last year's staff skit, which was outrageous, I was asked to ensure nothing too dodgy would be allowed and there would be NO repeat of last year's antics, quite right to!. Oh, the irony!

Dean K was the compare, items included:

Hippy Chicks -Danielle Nicola Kerry and Mrs P.

Tappin Turkeys (had to be seen to be believed) with Debbie, Amanda, Cheryl R, Suzanne, Belinda, Shelly H and Karen L.

Jim's jolly (get your key's out) sing-a-long rounded things off as usual. A great fun event to end the term!

32 – ROOM AT THE INN!

After Christmas, we returned to The Royal National Hotel. I, as a member of staff, now had to 'act' responsible and I mainly did but, for one incident which has lingered long in the memory!

Hotel security allowed for registered guests only to stay overnight, fair enough! When returning from the theatre I was pleased to see Craig K and John S who were visiting. Craig's brother Dean who had invited them back for a drink. One drink led to another so, when Dean asked if it was OK if Craig and John 'crash out on their room floor, I said,

"Yes but, keep the noise down to a dull roar and for goodness' sake, DON'T TELL ANYONE ELSE!"

No sooner had I just settled down for the night than my internal phone rang. It was the night manager.

"Mr Bradshaw, please can you meet me outside room." (Whatever Dean's room number was) "The room next door has complained of an unacceptable noise level!"

A couple of minutes later I followed my ears from whence the noise was emanating and met up with said night manager!

I offered to go in and sort it out but he was insistent in following me in!

Oh dear, the opening of the door was like that scene from the Marx Brothers film, *A Night at the Opera*, where someone opens the cabin door and twenty people fall out!

Word had gotten out; amongst the students that Craig and John were 'staying over'. It was all good fun but obviously I had to vouch for the fact they were all 'our students'(which in essence they were, or at least was!) I left John and Craig in there with his brother, whilst shooing everyone else out, including the actual residents of the room to make it look like John and Craig were our students!

Not sure where the other two slept, but just as I had reassured the night manager that, indeed they were all our students (he didn't ask whether they were past or present students so I wasn't telling any fibs!), I stepped out of the room with the manager behind me

I couldn't believe my eyes!

A bed was being carried towards the room by four girls (I think Nickie C and Claire P made up two of the culprits), one each corner with, would you believe it, another girl asleep in it! (Could have been Debbie C.)

Waving my hands frantically as if to say *get back, get back*, (as I couldn't speak with the night manager right behind me!).

I was able to engage him in some irrelevant 'chit chat' along the lines of,

"I don't think you'll have any further problems with our students tonight" and "I'm so sorry for the trouble."

"Oh, it's OK, we get this kind of thing all the time with students," said the night manager. I thought to myself, I bet you don't get beds being carried down the corridor on a regular occurrence! The chat was just long enough for the bed its contents and said girls to be returned to their rightful room!

Oh, the joys of 'being responsible'!

Next morning after 'as much toast as we could eat' we beat a hasty retreat! It was that hasty that Emma D and Marilena B, left their suitcases in the hotel reception, expecting the 'hired help' (coach driver or one of the staff!) to load it in, not realising they were 'without' until arriving back on the Fylde Coast!

Can you imagine the security alert at the hotel when two suspicious cases were left 'unattended'? It's a wonder a controlled explosion wasn't carried out!

33 – *BRIGHT LIGHTS* FINALE

Next up was our *Bright Lights* production at the Grand Theatre on Sunday the 1st March 92 and then two weeks later at The Charter Theatre Preston on Sunday 14th March.

Although we didn't know it at the time of performance, these were to be the 'finale' for *Bright Lights*.

The new BTEC did not allow for as much flexibility of timetable for staff or students as, outside course moderators had to verify course work to ensure due diligence.

This was time consuming, added to which, the cost of staging TWO major productions at a professional venue meant it now, in a new era of course budget restrain, not being not justifiable to our paymasters.

There was of course the obligatory 'dungarees' needed for the opening *Bright Lights* number and excerpts from our annual musical, *Pirates*! Glad to say *Bright Lights* went out with a bang.

34 – BEST IN SHOW, BUT WENDY'S NIGHTMARE!

Unless you have experienced the build up to a performance, it's difficult to describe the adrenalin rush just beforehand!

Rehearsals for *Pirates* were coming together. Most G&S (Gilbert and Sullivan) musicals have many strands to them, *Pirates* being the most stranded!

Alan was a great set designer and from the start had been involved with the production but, he was also busy with the continuing development of the ever-expanding department.

He brought in Pete Mulleny to help out with stagecraft. He slotted in straight away and had a great sense of humour, which endeared himself to the students!

Chorography was key. The college was blessed with, in my humble opinion, the best dance teacher I have ever known.

The very patient but creative Debbie Smyth. The work she did with the policemen (most of which, weren't the last bit of the word, except Andy C!) was without exception the best bit of choreography I have had the pleasure of witnessing. Debbie also choreographed the maidens, how she ever got them to behave as proper 'young ladies' was a miracle!

There have been plenty of others that have come close. Hot Box Dancers in Guys and Dolls and Chicago's Cell Block Tango to name but two!

Through Debbie, an extremely talented Australian called Peter Stamford was brought in. He had unique skills set, one of which was stage sword fighting, ideal for this production.

His contribution in teaching not just with the sword fights, but stage fights and acrobatics, gave this production so much life. More of Peter later as he came to establish himself as a firm favourite, especially with the students!

It was also a fine bit of directing for Angela Moran in her final college production. What a production to bow out on!

Jim was also on brilliant form, getting the best out of the entire cast, in this completely stylised production.

In fact, the whole production was spot on. It had a talented cast of principals especially, and in my humble opinion, two of the best singers in, Marilena B and Holly N and also the afore mentioned and brilliant Andy C but, chiefly the best principal performer in a role I ever saw at college, the outstanding Dean K as the Major General!

I have to confess I never saw *West Side Story*, which most students and staff who were involved in that say, it was THEE standout college production but, for me, *The NEW Pirates of Penzance* was my favourite college production.

All the elements worked perfectly together and I'll never forget one moment in particular when, Marilena sang 'Poor Wandering One', it made the hairs on the back of my neck stand on end!

Dean's 'rap' was also a standout moment. I can just imagine Jim on the first night of rehearsals with his orchestra, "Now then, we doing a G&S production this year" (a cheer goes up from the trained musicians!) "But, with a difference. There's a rap in it!" (Orchestra groans!) Not sure how but 'rap' they did!

A mention also for dear old Wendy, how she costumed so many different elements I do not know. Well, I do actually, as she wasn't backward at coming forward to let the students know at least, how little sleep she got, the nearer 'showtime' approached! Nevertheless, pirates, daughters, principals and policemen costumes, all made this production a stand out.

Even, on the face of it, G&S was not considered 'box office'. The selling the production was part of the students' curriculum and the fact that (to quote the G&S musical I was in at school) 'the sisters and the cousins and the aunts' came (as well as mums and dads) from miles around which made for a most enthusiastic audience and a production enjoyed by all concerned.

The entire Performing Arts staff and students can be immensely proud of this production. In my time there I think it was the most accomplished as there were so many different strands to bring together. Unless you a specialist in G&S its very difficult to; 'get to grips' with, but we did and the show was a great success.

Overall credit must go to Alan Evans, as it was not only his suggestion in the first place. He had the faith and trust in students and staff to pull it off, knowing it was his head on the block, if we didn't, especially considering the 'not insignificant cost' of staging it at prestigious The Grand Theatre!

35 – AFTER GLOW

Alan's boss was a great guy called Neville Wakling. He was so thrilled with the production he took the entire staff of Performing Arts out to Sunday lunch at the prestigious Clifton Arms in Lytham.

I felt somewhat of a 'young interloper' and teaching-wise, out of my depth. Neville held centre stage and toasted all the production staff, including Alan and of course Wendy who worked miracles with the costumes.

I honestly didn't expect any praise as my contribution was, to motivate students to market their own production. When Neville credited me with "the fantastic audiences" throughout the run I was slightly embarrassed and a little 'taken-aback' by the fulsome praise, in front of Brian and co, but acted suitably shy with this accolade!

It was that 'after show' meal that I think not only gave me the confidence to feel like I had arrived and belonged' with my mentors but, they had reciprocated by welcoming me aboard with 'open arms'. Thanks to Neville that day, I had to 'pinch myself' but I felt so proud to be appreciated and recognised by the very staff who had taught me the year before. Now I was one of them!

There followed that year, a great 'in-house' production from the first year in-take of the new BTEC Students, *Chicago*. We also did this later at the Grand. This show was ideal for students and although slightly risqué, it's a production both cast and audience enjoy and this first production was no exception.

Sadly, my short time as a lecturer in Journalism came to end. Kaye Keir gave me my first opportunity in teaching and I am eternal grateful to her for that. Kaye taught me many things but, something neither of us could have foreseen was sometimes how luck and coincidence play their part.

I remember to this day on returning to the staff room after one lesson to be greeted by John Barnett, owner of Radio Wave and journalist (and all-round good egg) Alister Clark also from the station. Kaye introduced me and the conversation went something like this:

John B - "Do you have any suitable trainee journalists or presenter DJ's who would be willing to come in and help"

I looked at Kaye, then without hesitation volunteered my services! Talk about being in the right place at the right time. I knew it was student help he meant but I wasn't going to let this opportunity go!

I did have it in mind anyway just to rock up at their front door and 'offer my services' but, on this occasion, opportunity knocked for me and I walked straight in the door!

I think I started the following week and stayed until the station ceased in September 2020. How I blagged it and, what the station had to put up with for twenty-eight years, was nothing short of miraculous. I put it down to another 'tour de force' of acting skills!

Radio Wave was where I belonged. I had so many amazing memories. What a book that would make! I will write it one day. Names most defiantly will need to be changed to protect the guilty! I was the luckiest and the happiest man alive in having jobs that I would have gladly paid to be there!

Back in Performing Art's, Alan rewarded me with an improved contract which I gratefully accepted.

I really enjoyed my first year 'acting' to be a teacher and without too many practical jokes being played. I was now acting like a responsible tutor and to that end my mentors taught me well!

What would the next academic year hold?

36 – A 'COCKEYED' OPTIMIST

When the 1992–93 year began, I was full of optimism. The department headed by Alan Evans with, Brian Hindle Head of Drama and Jim Thomas Head of Music, were fully supported by the rest of the staff.

This now included the afore mentioned Pete Stamford who was brought in to help with Arts Admin, where he got students to sign (because they hadn't read it properly) a contract saying they owed him a pint of beer! Always read the small print!

His morning warm-up classes became legendary, as he put poor 'hung over' students through their paces. These came to be known as 'Pete's Boot Camps'

Sadly we lost Peter at the end of 2021, but as the tributes have shown his 'legendary status' will live long in our memory!

An exceptional crop of talented students ensured that our reputation amongst the prestigious London-based drama schools gave everyone a sense we were producing the goods for what was needed for a career in this most competitive of industries.

This was already bearing fruit as the likes of former students Joanna Riding, David Thewlis, Josie Walker, Vicky Entwistle and more recently since I had been at college, John Simm Craig Kelly and David Royle were rising to the top.

On the West End stage, Joanna Riding won the Olivier award for best actress in a musical, *Carousel* Josie Walker was also in musicals in the West End. Dave Royle was stand-out in his film and TV roles Vicky Entwistle was in *Coronation Street* and John Simm was beginning to make it big time both on film and TV whist Craig Kelly had landed a role in the film *Titanic*!

It made my role somewhat easier as media outlets, especially the local and regional ones, who became aware of our 'hotbed of talent' and barely a week went by without one of the above having their latest offering reviewed!

When I said it made my role easier, part of what I was charged to do was to 'market the various courses' in drama, dance, and music. We took various productions into schools, creating awareness of what we offered and by having 'role models' at the top of their profession it gave an indication that, with hard work dedication talent (and much luck) they too could pursue, what now was perceived as a legitimate career in the 'creative and performance arts'!

37 – A SAD FAREWELL TO ANGELA MORAN

The timetable was now a lot different to when I was a student, however some of the 'Old Faithfull's still remained.

The Christmas Review saw a welcome return for *Hippychicks 2*, supplemented this year with Abba which was good fun with Tim R and three others! Once again hosted by your compere, Mr Dean K.

I have to say, although the review was up to its usually high standard it will always be remembered by me as, the last time I saw Angela Moran. For this wonderful, dedicated woman sadly died over the Christmas break that year. Angela had put a brave face on things and had done so for some time. I knew she wasn't well but had no concept of just how ill she was and it came as a tremendous shock when Brian, over the Christmas break, rang to tell me the sad news.

It left a void, which was so hard to fill. The out-pouring of emotion and grief at her funeral from past and present students was so moving.

Her name and reputation lived long in all who knew her, long after her passing.

38 – QUAKER OATS FOR THE HONEYMOON COUPLE!

It took a little time for the department to recover, but recover we did, onwards to London where it gave the students in particular a chance to let their 'hair down'.

I think one of the main reasons of the course's success was, the opportunities for students to see top quality theatre which, besides Broadway, was the best in the world.

Those West End performances then gave students the incentive to try and realize their ambitions., allied with the annual Grand Theatre production, it drove their incentive to achieve their life-times goals!

After returning from London the BTEC Second Year students were preparing to embark on their national tours! This was to prove an eye-opener, for all concerned, especially me!

Fancy putting me in charge of a group of students who were about to tour their final project. What possibly could go wrong!

So, mid-way through that term, off we went, touring the Caucasian Chalk Circle (don't ask!); one mini bus full of students, plus gullible driver followed by, stage truck with staff member and stage manager.

There is a well-known saying that, 'what goes on tour, stays on tour' and for the main it will, says he, whilst writing this and trying not to bite his lip!

In my defence I will say that the tour, including accommodation and food, was wholly organised by the students.

As well as performance roles, students had separate organisational roles and responsibilities, which would enable them to complete this all-important final 'touring project' successfully!

I think the lessons the staff learned from this (and by jove, we did) was that touring didn't necessarily mean a nationwide tour. All in all, most things went OK.

I know you are sensing a big but here!

The play was performed to the highest standards, every credit there. Unfortunately, the tour schedule was all over the place as venue dates could not always ensure a concise tight close together experience. It wasn't quite Cornwall to John O'Groats then Norwich followed by Swansea, but it wasn't far off!

As well as the zig zag tour itinerary, accommodation was to say the least basic. It was enough to put one of touring for life! Except for, the best experience of all, which was, for one overnight, somewhere in deepest Gloucestershire, at an old disused Quaker House.

The first thing on arrival we found out, there was no electric lighting or heating but oddly, electric power.

A shopping list for food and drink was made, to which candles and my suggestion of cling film were added and whilst one lot made the place habitable for the evening, I took the rest on a shopping expedition.

We dined well that evening, although I thought maybe the one vat of wine would have sufficed!

As darkness fell it was time for a bit good clean fun. Now where did they put that cling film?

Everyone was having a good old giggle, now was my chance. Sneaking into 'the ladies excuse me' and with fading light, I lifted the lid of the loo, put cling film over the entire area, put the seat back down, then returned the cling film to where I had taken it. I was to sit back down, without anyone blinking an eyelid then, waited for the first (and probably only victim).

Sure enough, before long, one of the girls picked up a candle and trundled off to the loo. From within the inner sanctum of trap two came a scream to waken the dead, that was heard by all who, then came a running!

Best gloss over the details but my name was prime suspect and because of the wine consumption everyone, including the now changed victim, took it in 'good spirits'.

We partied on into the night and as the responsible mini-bus driver I only had a couple of glasses of wine, not wanting to be 'over the limit' when travelling the following morning.

So, my memory of that evening, unlike others who had overindulged, are still quite vivid. Not wishing to be a kill joy, I do remember partaking in a slightly risqué game of 'truth or dare'. I would like to state here and now there was nothing untoward, just a blooming good laugh, but I do urge the person (I know who you are) with the picture of me, to do the decent thing. I do have my reputation to think of!

Eventually the evening wound down. We had two separate large sleeping quarters in this creaky old house in which to sleep. Think there was only three lads, including myself, but several girls so they quite naturally they had the larger room. It was quite evident that one or two of them were 'nervous' about having no lights and 'creaking' noises from all over the house. I didn't help matters by suggesting the house "may be haunted!"

I think one or two of you, knowing me by now, are ahead of me! I waited until all was quiet, before sneaking outside, climbing on the roof then stamping about, hoping to cause panic below. Maybe the roof was a little more soundproof than I thought, couldn't think of another reason why panic hadn't ensued below, could you?

The reason soon became clear. One of the boys (who shall not remain nameless) had heard me sneak out and climb on the roof, informed the girls what I was up to and then, in a final act of double-crossing, locked me out.

I was left outside in the perishing cold for what seemed like an eternity. Thanks, Robin G!

I redeemed myself somewhat the following morning. I had a clear head where others were slow to exit their pit. Robin, had been held in high esteem and every credit to him, for thinking to pack a toaster.

I also thought outside the box and packed a screwdriver. I had plenty of time to unscrew the plug and remove the fuse, before sneaking back in my sleeping bag!

In due course, bleary-eyed, we all ensembled the kitchen. "Robin, it's taking ages for the toast, it doesn't seem to be working."

"Stand back let me sort it."

Much frustration, up and down with the lever, didn't make a jot of difference. I proffered a suggestion that "it could be the fuse; it may have slipped out!"

No one even clicked when I offered Robin my screwdriver to check if it was indeed 'the fuse'. The look of surprise on his face when he couldn't quite believe his eyes. There was no fuse!

Holding the fuse aloft I said, "Oh I have spare one here."

Expletives were much overused in this house of God. Retribution had been achieved and to coin one of Jim's phrases: 'We had as much toast as we wanted.'

There was one situation that I haven't alluded to, but as I mentioned earlier, what went on tour, stayed on tour and I can't just bring to mind their names anyway!

The stage truck, its driver and the stage manager arrived quite late that evening so it was extremely courteous of them to set up their own 'honeymoon suite' so not to disturb the rest of us. Well, that was their reasoning at least!

39 – KISS ME, KATE

Back at college, rehearsals without the second-year touring students for the Grand Theatre production were well advanced for *Kiss Me, Kate*.

Once again, we had a great cast, shouldn't really single people out but, some outstanding leads including Suzanne M, Gavin A, Anna D and an upcoming future TV performer, Craig P, who even then, had great stage presence!

There was a lovely dedication on the first page of that year's programme which read:

'This production is dedicated to ANGELA MORAN, a well-loved and much respected colleague and friend.'

That last bit of being a friend was so true; no one did more than Angela to help students, she even put them up in her house.

The genre of the production was difficult for young students to grasp, but Angela Hudson, Jim Thomas and Debbie Smyth worked miracles in getting superb performances out of a talented cast as did Brian with the Shakespeare aspect of this double pronged production!

Once again, we said goodbye to some talented students at the end of the summer term but, chuffed that some had made it to prestigious drama schools and knowing, as with previous generations, it wouldn't be that long before they turned up on the box or, on stage and film. The reputation that Brian Hindle had created as the go-to 'foundation course' had certainly borne fruit and was continuing to flourish!

40 – FIDDLING THE AUDITIONS

The production line rolled into action once again in September 1993, with a new crop of 'wannabes'.

First question they all wanted to know: what show are we performing next May?

Eyebrows were raised once again when Alan's suggestion of *Fiddler on The Roof* was mooted! Once looked into, the potential for the students doing it justice made it the favourite from that year's short list!

Again, a difficult one for students to get to grips with.

Auditions, which consisted of a dramatic piece and a song were great fun. Not I might add for the nervous students, keen to impress but, for me at least, to be treated to an array of auditions which, in the main showed just what talented potential we had.

Sometimes difficult to watch as, occasionally nerves got the better of one or two but, to give them credit they battled through which, again showed their determination to succeed and impress.

I had auditioned by this time many a Christmas Review but, this was different casting for a lead role in our annual production so maybe on reflection, from my point of view, sitting there with a smirk on my face for some of the more outlandish auditions was, not very professional, but the sheer joy of seeing something out of the ordinary performed was wonderful.

Anna D and Martin N stood out and were cast in the lead roles but some surprizing auditionee's were

- Rachel I ('Memory' from *Cats* and a good reading)
- Verity T ('Can't Help Lovin That Man of Mine' from *Showboat*)
- Eira I *(Chorus Line)*

Kate F and Craig P, who both later went on to be big stars of the small screen (Kate, a stalwart in *Coronation Street as Tracy Barlow* and Craig in *Misfits*, *White Chapel* and more recently *Line Of Duty*) auditioned but for some reason, did not shine through. They undeniably had wonderful stage presence, especially the latter. Kate was a great all-rounder; her acting and dancing were brilliant and she had a lovely voice.

Essentially, it's a musical about oppressed Jews living in Russia in 1905 and the enduring 'human spirit' they had surviving in the face of adversity. Subject-wise the most difficult musical, bar none, that the Performing Arts students were asked to understand and perform.

Alan wouldn't have chosen it if he didn't think the students could pull it off. He had a vision of how it would look and for the one and only time in our Grand Theatre productions, he played a major role in how the cast shaped up. With calibration of both Brian and Angela directing and Jim and Debbie the students were in 'safe hands', ensuring the 'character and delivery' were brought out and with the sombre tone needed.

41 – AREN'T STAGE WEIGHTS HEAVY!

It's funny, my student days I can remember vividly, but my teaching time, which lasted a lot longer, from 1993–2001, I can only recall the most outstanding events and as a 'responsible tutor' my practical jokes days were mainly behind me, apart from one or two opportunities I could not resist!

Along with events, certain students from down the years I recall distinctly, not necessary, those whose acting stood out. Some also had great personalities and were a good laugh!

The problem for me was the longer the students were at college, the more they got to know my sense of humour!

Fiddler on the Roof was performed in May 1994 at the Grand Theatre and despite, once again, outstanding performances by the cast, the one abiding memory of *Fiddler* was in the scene where two 'characters' should be seen to be struggling to carry their life-long possessions in a trunk on their long trek to their new homeland, weary, downtrodden and exhausted!

Instead, they, nightly, one at each end, just picked up this 'featherlight' trunk and briskly walked across stage without a care in the world!

Something needed to be added to the trunk to make the scene more realistic!

Aren't stage weights heavy!

The two students (let's just say for name's sake we call them Emma W and Suzanne M) were completely oblivious to the fact that I, along with a stagehand, lifted two extremely heavy stage weights into the trunk before sliding it into position for them to carry across stage, surely this time it would look more realistic!

Not only could they not pick it up, it took all their strength and energy just for them both to shove it across stage. Talk about having a sweat on after reaching the other side! It certainly added a touch of realism to the scene!

I can still picture them to this very day trying to shove the thing, whilst all around were wondering why, all of a sudden, they appeared to be not only 'upstaging' but 'milking it' for all they were worth!

They knew exactly who caused them this unnecessary sweatage and I received a suitable ear-bashing but, it was worth it and I must admit, apart from the black eye, they did take it in good spirits.

42- A FLAME THAT STILL BURNS BRIGHT!

Normally the summer term after the show was a bit anti-climatical but, this summer was to prove very special!

After a road trip to France a couple of years earlier, Jim Thomas, with his brother Dave, retraced the steps that Joan of Arc took on her crusade across France, Jim was so inspired by this he wrote a musical based on her life. He titled it *JEANNE D'ARC*

He assembled the cream of local Am Dram performers along with some hand-picked students from college. What a cast, but it was lacking a powerful young actress to play the lead role, who to turn too?

Jim had stayed in touch with a former protégé of his, Joanna Riding who, back in the mid-eighties was an exceptional student and standout performer in The Grand Theatre productions.

In 1993, she had won a prestigious Olivier award for Best Actress in a Musical for her role as Julie Jordan in *Carousel* at The National Theatre.

I, along with Jim, in '93, took an extra London Theatre trip that summer to see her in that award-winning role.

The whole production was superb and its star's performance that night was, the best I'd ever seen.

Jim arranged to meet up with her in Theatre Bar after her exhausting performance for a quiet drink. It was then Jim plucked up the courage to ask her if she could take on this 'historic role' the following summer of '94.

Honoured though Jo was to have been asked by her mentor, she could not give an immediate answer as she was still contracted to *Carousel* and unsure of her professional commitments further down the line so, could not say yes there and then, which Jim fully understood!

Still Jo was thrilled to see Jim. I felt like a lemon as they both exchanged anecdotes for over an hour!

By this time, it had gone midnight and 'gallant' as Jim was, he offered to escort Jo home, which was a good forty-five minutes' walk away.

About half way Jo stopped and suggested we go into a small bar where there was 'live' music. We found a table and Jim and Jo began to once again reminisce, until their chat was interrupted by the compere saying, "We have Joanna Riding in tonight. Jo, will you come up and sing?"

Without batting an eyelid, unrehearsed, she picked up the microphone and delivered 'The Girl from Ipanema' perfectly!

After we had escorted Jo back to her flat, we arrived back in our hotel room. I looked at my watch,2.30 a.m. I said to Jim, "Did all that just happen?" What an evening!

Jo, true to her word, phoned Jim at home. I'm not sure of the exact conversation but it was along the lines of, "Jim, I have some good news for you, I am free to play the lead role in *JEANNE D'ARC*" I know Dave, Jim's brother, was there as well when the call came through and to say they were both ecstatic was, a gross understatement!

What an incentive for the cast, to be on stage with one the West End's leading lights who was 'coming home' to perform!

Rehearsals took place from '93 to performance date in '94 and everyone pulled together. Jim's brother Dave Thomas, was 'instrumental' throughout the entire production and deserves the upmost credit for his inspiring contribution.

He accompanied Jim on his road trip to France and help score the musical. He was brilliant during rehearsal.

The college staff also got 'fully onboard' with it. Debbie, as usual, with her impeccable chorography. Alan helping with the staging and set. Brian and Angela helping build the characters but, it was Wendy I felt most for who, was left scratching her head with sorting medieval French costumes.

I remember asking her once if she was OK (fatal!). I got chapter and verse about her staying "I was up all night sewing monks' habits!"

I helped with marketing the production. I must admit selling this new musical based on an 'historic heroine' was an immense challenge, one I met with fortitude and I am glad to say, I managed to attract a lot of media attention, especially now we had Joanna as our leading light (pun intended!).

We knew we had a great production. All the ingredients were there: a leading actress, the cream of local talent as well as hand-picked students, but, most of all an exceptional musical!

Hand-picked talent included stage manager Neil Thompson from the Grand, who created the most realistic finale (the burning at the stake).

The Performing Art staff pulled out all the stops, in fact we got the full support of the college.

I'm not just saying this because of my friendship with Jim, but this was the most incredible score of ANY musical I have ever seen.

If you don't believe me then take a listen to the soundtrack CD. All the music is brilliant but, stand-out tracks PUT YOUR HAND ON YOUR HEART and DID I DO WRONG other great songs included The Sound Of Dreams, If I Could Ask, Don't Hide Behind A Painted Smile, Fly On The Wall and Can I Be The Man.

These songs were beautiful crafted, from the heart and were woven into the fabric of a truly wonderful production!

In everything but name this was truly a 'professional production' and should have been a big West End theatre hit!

We actually did get the opportunity to perform it the West End, when several years later, we work-shopped it at The Dominion Theatre when Ben Elton's *We Will Rock You* was at full blast!

The Proscenium Theatre Company performed at the Grand Theatre from Wednesday 29th June – Saturday 2nd

July 1994 for which I co-opted some reliable front-of-house (FOH) staff (and Emma W).

I am struggling to put into words my feeling and have come over all unnecessary as my thoughts drift back to that run.

I mentioned earlier that up until I'd seen Joanna Riding star in *Carousel* that was the best performance I had ever seen. Well, now her performance in *JEANNE D'ARC* had surpassed it.

It wasn't just Jo's performance, even though she 'lived' the part. The whole production was stand out.

On the last night, my FOH team watched the performance from the Royal Box. The emotion of the finale on the final night got to us. Tears filled our eyes as we watched the curtain fall, for me, I knew I had witnessed my GREATEST EVER EXPERIENCE IN THE THEATRE.

Nearly thirty years later, even though I attend the Grand Theatre almost weekly (apart from the dreaded 'C' word interrupting for eighteen month's) and have performed twice there in The National Theatre's production of *An Inspector Calls* not to mention my love of *The Woman in Black*, I still think back to Saturday 2nd July 1994, as my 'greatest ever' theatre experience, so I say, 'Thank you for the music', Jim, it will live within me forever!

That experience was just the start of *Jeanne D'Arc*, the musical. Although Joanne Ridding never reprised her role because of her professional commitments, there were several other performances of the production including, the following year at The Charter Theatre Preston with Jennifer W as lead.

A year later Jim, Neil Thompson and I took a reckie trip to The Edinburgh Fringe Festival to look for a suitable venue to perform the musical. We found the ideal venue so with, the entire cast, crew and orchestra we took our own road trip the following year to perform *Jeanne D'Arc* at the prestigious St Giles' Cathedral on The Royal Mile, with Helen R in the lead role.

There have also been performances at the aforementioned Dominion Theatre in the West End, Cartmel Priory in the Lakes, St Paul's in Marton and St John's Minster in Preston.

I am so proud to have been involved in this production. You would think, in the overall scheme of things, writing the musical would be the most difficult part however, despite many years of 'lobbying' the great and the good of theatre producers including, Jim writing to Cameron Macintosh who, wrote back to say if he wasn't involved at that time with *Martin Gere* (then a fairly new production) and having *Les Mis* in full swing, but he thought three 'French historic' productions at the same time would be too much!

In my humble opinion, without doubt, this was the best musical ever, never to have had the acclaim it deserves. One day maybe, one day, it still could happen! I still play the CD regularly, Did I Do Wrong?

43 – THE CLIFTON DRIVE TAKEOVER

When term recommenced in September 1994 the usual buzz of anticipation that accompanied a new intake of students was still clearly evident.

Alan had to look at expanding teaching space. Our reputation and success were rapidly becoming recognised nationally and teaching space was at a premium!

This was now a 'centre of excellence' where viable careers could be accessed. I had witnessed back in the day, at tutorial, when Brian had been outspoken about career teachers in school, who, back then did not value, recognise or even worse, have any concept of just what valuable and diverse careers there were in the performance arts!

Now courses in music, music technology, media, dance, drama stage craft and stage make-up were now all accessible and available. Even students who hadn't achieved academically at school could do a one year foundation course in order to peruse their hopes and ambitions.

Where to house all these students? First for the chop, we lost our beloved proscenium arch theatre, in order to make room for more teaching space. Then, over time, as the academic courses gradually relocated to Bispham and Palatine (later known as Central Campus) we took over the entire Clifton Drive campus!

Former art rooms and academic classrooms were adapted into performance and teaching spaces. Even the old gym was converted into a lovely sprung floor dance studio!

I must admit, it was less intimate and more like a production line. The ratio of our successes did slow, mainly because completion of the BTEC also enabled student progression to universities as well as the well-trodden and prestigious London Theatre schools which, financially were becoming out of reach, with little, or no council grants and fewer bursaries from the actual establishments!

The industry itself was also rapidly changing, so training for viable industry jobs was essential. Performance colleges and centres of excellence were springing up everywhere to rival ours.

Thanks to the wonderful Brian Hindle ably supported by the rest of the staff, our reputation was maintained and our courses had the 'house full' sign up!

When Brian first started the course, it was the only one in the North West, students like John Simm and Joanna Riding came from all over Lancashire. We had to guard against complacency as now other performing arts centre's such as Burnley were able to offer similar opportunities also with progression into university!

44 – SHOW OF SHOWS

Back at the coalface that year's production was chosen. *Guys and Dolls* which, had been originally performed back in 1987 and was such a great student vehicle.

After the Christmas Review, as sure as night follows day, came the London Trip. I had to pretend to be a strict tutor and could hardly keep a straight face when Jim and I were called to a 'fracas' at around two in the morning involving a student dare.

Four of our lads were running naked (apart from their socks) down the corridor. A large West Indian lady was disturbed by the noise and on opening the door in her nightie (funny place for a door!), was confronted by the boys in their 'birthday suits.' She was that shocked. she nearly had a stroke (but couldn't reach!)

"Would you recognise them, if you saw them again?" the lady was asked by the night manager.

"Only if they wore the same socks!" came the reply!

We had to act promptly. Our stay there (and other things) were dangling by a thread! The Manager wasn't best pleased so, to ensure we all didn't get kicked out, the following morning we dispatched the guilty party (who shall remain nameless) back home on the train.

I had many memorable London moments down the years including, going to the theatre with Angela Hudson arranging tickets for a Noel Coward play (I think it was *Private Life's*) We arrived at the theatre in plenty of time and found our seats ten minutes before curtain up. To our surprise a couple also presented their tickets for exactly the same seats. The house manager was called who agreed that we were indeed sat in the correct seats, on the right date. Unfortunately though, we were in the wrong theatre and had to leg it next door just in time for the performance!

I also saw for the first time, some wonderful performances including *The Woman in Black* and with Jim a great farce called *Don't Dress for Dinner*.

On another memorable London visit I think, the following year, again with Jim, also Yvonne and for some reason that escapes me, a student (LB) tagged along. We went to see a comedy at The Queens Theatre called *Laughter on the 23rd Floor*.

The play, staring one of my all-time favourite comic screen actors, Gene Wilder, recounted how some of the great American screen actors and comedians, back in the fifties, wrote weekly ninety minutes scripts for Sid Caesar's *Your Show of Shows* which went out live to sixty million people across America.

Woody Allen, Mel Brooks, Carl Reiner, Neil Simon and Larry Gelbart (creator of *M*A*S*H*) were some of the well-known names who cut their teeth on this massive American hit that I don't think was ever shown in this country!

Gene Wilder had worked with a few of them, notably for Woody Allen on *Everything You Want to Know About Sex* (The scene where Gene falls in love with a sheep is hilarious- honest!) and also, most famously with Mel Brooks, on *Young Frankenstein*, one of my 'all-time favourite American comedies'.

So, you could imagine my delight when, an hour before 'curtain up', I interviewed the great man himself, not just about the play, but his life on stage and screen. Chuffed was an understatement!

It never ceases to amaze me, that despite the 'big bucks' on offer from the American film industry, just how many renowned performers prefer to work on stage. Gene Wilder was such a person!

I still have the theatre ticket but 'god knows' what happened to my interview. Perhaps I dreamt it!

Jim and I loved those theatre visits and we often recall some of the great productions we have seen down the years especially, as they were known back then, as The Whitehall Farces.

In fact, Jim and I talked about writing one called, Zip Up Your Doo Dah's Perhaps now with more time on our hands we should!

45 – THE RISE AND RISE OF PERFORMING ARTS...AND ALL THAT JAZZ!

The shows at the Grand continued. For the second time the college put on in 1995 *Guys and Dolls*. Great fun!

We had a great cast for this including Ben H, Nicola P, James N and Lorraine B but, in truth the entire cast were outstanding.

Also, in September of that year a new two-year HND (Higher National Diploma) university qualification course was introduced with Lisa Adams being brought in to run it with Alan.

This course was the equivalent to doing the first year of a degree and enabled those who successfully completed the course to go on to university, should they so wish!

For me, the best thing about the course was the diversity of the students which brought with them their regional dialects from across the country.

There was one slight snag, with them being a little older and wiser they were not as gullible and therefore practical jokes were kept to a minimum.

As marketing was a key and core part of the course the HND students not only took on roles in marketing the major ND annual production at the Grand Theatre but, also, through their own initiatives, were able to fund raise in able to stage their own productions at the world-famous 'Edinburgh festival'.

Jim and I went up a couple of times to see them perform. Some even tried their hand at 'stand-up' comedy, where the audience I think were professional hecklers! The sight of them being hauled off stage by a hook was most amusing. One guy (not one of our students I hastened to add) was still arguing with a heckler as he was slowly dragged off stage via a hook round his neck, oh the joys of stand-up comedy!

It was hard to think that in just a few short years how the college Performing Arts courses had exploded.

From humble beginnings in 1969 when Brian Hindle first started the foundation course on his own, to the mid-nineties when around 200 students and around twenty full and part-time staff worked there, made this one of top sought after courses in the country!

Also, during this period, the department continued to provide top class actors for the profession. Craig Parkinson, Kate Ford and Jodie Prenger being the most well-known but, hundreds more in supporting roles in film stage and TV.

The production in May 1996, (June 6th–8th) turned out to be one of the best the college staged. *Chicago*. Initially it was Alan's brainwave. Angela, Jim and Debbie pulled out all the stops to stage a wonderfully directed, choreographed and performed production. Yes, it was a bit risqué for young people to perform in not much clothing and although the theme was quite 'adult' it was in the main 'tongue in cheek', apart from the 'Cell Block Tango'. Dear oh dear, not for the faint-hearted. I still have the production shots and have promised Tracy B, I would not sell them on to Playboy!

Because of the amount of the students, for the first time since Grand Theatre productions started, we staged two productions.

Brian directed the first of two Shakespeare productions, *Twelfth Night*, which was a real challenge, both for him and the students but, Brian being Brian, got some great performances out of an enthusiastic cast!

Two years later in 1998 he had an even bigger challenge with *A Midsummer Night's Dream*, one of the most popular, therefore the most known and loved with the audience, so getting it right was crucial! Needless to say, he did!

That year our musical production was another bash at Gilbert and Sullivan, this time with the *Hot Mikado*, both productions were staged at the theatre from 10th–13th June 1998.

46 - THE SHOWS GO ON… AND ON… UNTIL!

My later years, though nonetheless enjoyable, do tend to merge with one another. Teaching to a set syllabus, made it difficult from year to year to distinguish the day-to-day running of the course so, highlights and memories of those later years tend to revolve round productions at the Grand and for a 'one off' (1997) at The Pavilion Theatre within The Winter Gardens complex.

To quote a famous nursery rhyme, we had so many students we didn't know what to do!

It was decided, in the year of our Lord 1997, to stage THREE major productions and students were encouraged to audition for one of them. The productions were staged between the 27th – 31st May.

The three very different productions were

- *CABARET*: directed and choreographed by Debbie, musical director Jim. Once again, an outstanding performance by Emma K as Sally Bowles. Great bit of casting in, Darren W in the girl's orchestra!

- *ALICE IN WONDERLAND*: directed by Brian and Angela. Claire C played the lead. She was, and still is, a great little actress

- *WESTENDERS*: directed by Yvonne. This was an all singing, all dancing show with excerpts from West End musicals, hence the show's title of *Westenders* (yes you are right, twas my idea to call it that!). A terrific cast with students belying their tender years to turn in outstanding performances. Stand out for me were, Jaymz N, Ben H, Ebby J, Allison B and Cassie C.

I know where my sympathies would have laid. I wonder how many nights poor Wendy was up sewing for THREE ENTIRLY DIFFERENT PRODUCTIONS!

If I'm honest The Pavilion Theatre within the Winter Gardens complex was not the ideal venue.

For one, we had been spoilt at The Grand. To perform at one of Countries leading theatre's and afforded all the luxuries a professional company had, made it for most students the pinnacle of their Performing Arts course

The Pavilion Theatre on the other hand had fallen into disrepair so needed some tlc to bring it up to performance spec. I could go into detail but let's just say the staff and students made the best of the situation and staged three top notch productions.

College productions had taken place at The Grand Theatre for over ten years but the cost of staging productions there had meant we needed to make a stand and show our hosts there were other performance spaces in which to give our talented students the public opportunity to shine!

Mission accomplished, the following year, we were back at The Grand!

As I mentioned earlier, in 1998, the college musical was *The Hot Mikado*. Of all the musical's the college have produced over many years for me, including, *The Boyfriend,* this seemed the least inspiring for students, but at least we were back at our natural home, The Grand Theatre.

In my humble opinion the G&S songs in *The Mikado* were not up to their usual standard. Our previous attempt, *(The New) Pirates of Penzance* was a fantastic production!

No fault what-so ever can be laid at the cast's door. As, with every single year, there was always exceptional talent and this year was no exception.

Emma B, Maurice T and Jodie P deserve special mentions as does Ebby J. All the staff once again put their heart and soul into it. I just think the vehicle was wrong. Still once again the students had this 'Once (or twice) in a lifetime' opportunity to perform at The Grand Theatre, which some would give their right arm for (left for me!)

Our final Grand Theatre productions were from 5th–7th June 1999. *Fame* directed by Yvonne Coverdale, with Jim as musical director and *The Lion, the Witch and the Wardrobe*, directed by Brian, Debbie and Angela.

Although this was to be the final curtain call for our productions, we couldn't complain, as the department had had the opportunity to perform at one of the country's leading theatres since 1985. Fifteen straight years and for some of those years we also performed *Bright Lights*. They may have been the last productions but, ironically a first for me, I actually chose one of the productions, citing 'bums on seats' for the children's C.S. Lewis classic.

It actually wasn't till six years later, in 2005, that the feature film was released and *The Chronicles of Narnia* especially *The Lion The Witch and The Wardrobe* became popular again. So, with a little foresight on my part (and also undeniably, a little sentimentality!) I reintroduced, to the good folk of The Fylde Coast, an old childhood favourite of mine. Pity at the time I didn't copyright the idea as now, the blooming thing is toured all over the country Hey Ho!

Performing Arts students throughout the ages never cease to amaze me. The casts for both productions were as wonderful as they had ever been. Yes, the faces had changed but the enthusiasm for performing, especially at the Grand Theatre, was as great as ever!

Louise W, Chris J and of course Shari R in Fame and Emma B, Richard R (and I suppose I better mention Leanne S or she'll bash me up) in *The Lion, the Witch and the Wardrobe*.

Unique to this production, I thought it may be a good idea to get a student's 'personal' perspective and insight as to what it was like from audition, to performance to run a weekly diary.

I chose, not just a lead performer, Louise W but, also a chorus member, Kym A. The 'local paper' *The Evening Gazette* (as it was back then) ran a weekly diary page to chart the progress of Louise and Kym stories in the build up to 'show time'.

It worked a treat, not only giving an insight as to what it was like being involved in the student's major production but, by the time of the performance, it had created local interest which, in turn, not only boosted bums on seats for the run but, also it gave potential students insight and inspiration, as to course content.

As usual at the end of a run of our annual Grand Theatre productions, there was much weeping and a wailing, heightened this time in the knowledge of it being our final ever performance there!

The students were not the only one's sheading a tear that night, I did to, knowing it was the end of an era for the department. Big changes were on the way!

47 – CLIFTON DRIVE, THE FINAL CURTAIN

The main reason these were to be the last ever productions at the Grand Theatre had become evident twelve months earlier when the college decided to 'consolidate' its buildings and Clifton Drive Campus was to be sold.

I have to say, it was a hard sell by Alan to the established staff, including myself, but especially Brian, Jim, Angela, Debbie and Wendy who, without putting to finer point on it, had invested their lives at Clifton Drive.

Time moves on though and the building was now 'bursting at the seams' with courses and students. Basically, not only was it not fit for purpose it was also in need of major repair!

Part of the success of Clifton Drive I think was that, we were allowed the autonomy and a 'free reign.' Even when Alan came in and even through his boss and head of site Neville Wakling, they allowed us to develop as they recognised Performing Arts students were a special breed (and a bit noisy at times and should be kept away from 'normal people')

Brian, who started it all, was instrumental in ensuring that through personal development, using performance as a base, we could enjoy learning the 'life skills' that enabled us to go on and be what we wanted to be! Even in jobs and careers that were not performance based!

I know I thanked you in life, Brian, for want you did for me, but here in print I would like to say, if it wasn't for you and all the other 'influential' staff including Alan, Jim, Angela M and Angela H, Debbie and Wendy I wouldn't have achieved as much professionally in my line of work without your help and support!

THANK YOU!

In the end, sad as it was, to leave Clifton Drive Campus a new purpose-built theatre, dance studios and rehearsal spaces were designed at Central Campus, to take the college into the new millennium, well September 1999 to be precise.

Before we moved, I organised a big reunion for all students since Brian started the 'foundation course' in 1969 upon till 1998.

Brought a tear to my eye (again) to see so many old friends and former students, many of which I'm still in touch with come back, one last time, to the place where it all started. Many happy memories were rekindled that day, people exchanging numbers and contact details.

All the staff, but especially Brian, enjoyed hearing stories of old and catching up with what ex-students were up to. I think we had to be 'chucked out' by the caretaker as none of us wanted that day to end.

Still, to this day, reunions are arranged and it is testament to not just the courses and tutors but also the building itself, that people hold that time in their live as I've heard so many describe it as, 'the best years of our lives'. No argument from me there!

48 – PASTURES NEW

September 1999 saw us firmly entrenched in our new surrounding of Central Campus, the main campus for Art and Design, another highly renowned course with students from all over the world coming to study.

I felt sorry for last year's intake who started at Clifton Drive and then found themselves at Central. It wasn't what they had signed up for. Young people are 'if nothing, but resilient' and they, unlike the staff, soon settled in to their new home!

Yes, there were teething problems; for example, the theatre was behind in completion which was a double whammy as not only was there nowhere to perform, but it also doubled as a teaching space which we were now short of, ironically one of the reasons why we moved in the first place!

Poor Alan, who was tearing his hair out in trying to get things right for us all in the department.

I can't pretend there wasn't resistance from the staff, not least in the fact that the staff rooms were separated.

Jim, myself and other music staff in one room, with Brian, Angela, Wendy and Yvonne in another and the dance staff downstairs, in yet another!

Eventually 'normal service' (whatever that was) resumed and much noise emanated from various rooms.

Complaints about the noise came, not just from the tranquillity and serenity of the Art department but also from the two streets that backed on to our performance space. Good!

Admittedly, a culture shock for the calm staff and art students; not their fault, nor the fault of our poor new neighbours but for sure there was no chance of us 'keeping quiet'. Making noise is what we do best!

49 GULLABLE AN YET, SATISFIED DJ

I had, back at Clifton Drive, been asked to devise a DJ training course to cover all aspects of that branch of the entertainment industry which had served me well from adolescence. It's what I did best and time to put something back!

I duly set out a curriculum which had THREE MAIN COMPONENTS:

- MOBILE DJ – I ran my own mobile DJ agency and naively thought, if there were any talented young people, I may be able to utilise them.
- CLUB DJ – Usually a less verbal presentation style but highly reliant on mixing one piece of music into another.
- RADIO PRESENTATION – A completely 'unique' style of presentation and one, since 1992, I had been fortunately been involved in at Radio Wave.

I found out before the first cohort arrived that the funding for the course had not only excluded 'all abilities' but it turned out it was a course for those, how can I put this politely, a course for VERY naughty boys (and one naughty girl!)

My patience was tested to the extreme, as these young people had had no formal education, had poor communication skills and had many complex social issues.

The only thing these 'rough diamonds' had in common was their passion for their own unique genre of MUSIC. (I had then no idea there were so many strands to Rap) Through music they were able to open up and took me into their confidence and sometimes their complex world!

I felt more like a social worker than a Performing Arts teacher. I ended up fighting their corner when things went wrong in their lives. It certainly gave me a realism and different prospective on life as well as opening up my mind to new musical strands. They were teaching me!

Looking back at all my achievements on the teaching side, this course and how these young people warmed, not only to it but, me as their mentor, gave me immense satisfaction. I had been able to turn a light switch on that mainstream education had failed them in

I was determined, to give these students an opportunity to learn a skill that could set them on a even path and that could even lead to a career in something that engaged them!

I cannot describe the self-satisfaction and sheer enjoyment etched on their faces, as the course developed, learning a skill and receiving a qualification. Chuffed would be an understatement!

It lies within all of us to be 'good at something'; not everybody is good at Maths and English (including me, I once spelt officiate… a fish e ate).

I had a couple of 'industry' successes. One young lad (Damian) went on to work in Japan and other far-flung countries for the Ministry of Sound and wrote me lovely letters and emails thanking me for my input enabling him to 'achieve his ambition'. The main success of the course was, for some, a 'light bulb' moment!

Despite horrendous challenges, this was a proud moment for me, not only testing my teaching skills but, my ability as a social worker!

Judging others without full knowledge of their circumstances is something we have all been guilty of and I was no exception!

50 – STUDENT OF THE YEAR... ONE LAST JAPE!

As the new Millennium dawned, Performing Arts was going from strength to strength. I felt so lucky to involved in such a vibrant place of work, where every day there was a new challenge. I had to pinch myself that for over ten years now both as student and now staff member I loved 'being there' however I sensed nothing this good could last forever and sooner or later 'a change was going to come'! I wish I wasn't so perceptive!

The 2000 London trip went ahead that year and as usual 'a good time was had by all' but unfortunately, one of the bedrocks that was synonymous with the course ceased.

As I mentioned previously, after fifteen glorious years the curtain came down on the Grand Theatre Productions!

The new intake, who only knew their new surrounding and had not had that opportunity to perform at The Grand Theatre so didn't know any different. However, the second years did and although we now had our own brand-new spanking theatre for us to perform in, but for 'old traditionalists' though, (i.e., the staff!) it wasn't quite the same.

Alan put his heart and soul into it. Not only was there a greater opportunity for students to perform productions but the central location meant 'marketing opportunities' were greater too. We even attracted touring companies eager to perform in Blackpool.

One event the college hosted was, their 'annual student of the year' awards which encompassed all campuses and students across Blackpool and the Fylde College. It was hosted and attended by the principalship and civic dignitaries.

I couldn't let this opportunity pass without a little jape!

As it befell me to organise 'front-of-house' for this prestigious event, I had quite naturally a list of award winners from across all the courses the college had to offer. I noted that the overall 'student of the year' had exactly the same name as one of our own Performing Art's students The tad gullible but, a good laugh none the same, Natalie A. She was a great student and we got on well and I wouldn't have let her fall in to the trap if I didn't think she would take it well.

I found said student, showed her the list of winners, with her name on the list and right on cue she took her place with a couple of her mates, where I placed them, at the back of the theatre her basking in the glory of what was to come. How it never crossed her mind as to WHY she should remotely be chosen as student of the year, beggars belief!

Unfortunately, unbeknownst to her, all the winners had already taken their seats on the front row for easy access to the stage

Cue principal of the college "And the winner of student of the year goes to… Natalie A." Our Natalie gets up from her seat at the back and, in her big clunking shoes starts to make her way down the gangway to the stage, only to see on arrival there, the real recipient of the award collect her trophy and sit back down. Beetroot I think can best describe her shade of red!

After a verbal volley of expletives she did eventually see the funny side to it, despite her embarrassment. Not just in front of the assembled throng, but once word had got out, to the rest of the performing arts students! I think she was also reprimanded for being in an awards ceremony to which she wasn't invited! Game gal though, took it well!

51 - NOTHING GOOD LASTS FOREVER!

I mentioned earlier a sense of foreboding. I must admit I never saw the bombshell after we returned from Christmas break in 2001 when Alan informed us all of his intention to leave at the end of the academic year.

He was instrumental in driving the department forward and although Brian was still having enormous success delivering at 'the coal face' he was not the natural successor to Alan as it would have taken him away from 'the classroom'. It would be a new appointment and although I have never feared change, I did fear someone coming in and recking what had been built up over many years.

It was therefore with much sadness we not only said goodbye to Alan but, to the Performing Arts Department as we knew it.

It was obvious from the start of that academic year, in September 2001 that the newly appointed Head wanted to stamp his own mark on the department, (fair enough) but the way he went about dismantling what we had built up was unforgivable!

Not being from that background he also had little knowledge or understanding of the different 'type of animal' performing arts students were.

His main aim I believe (maybe aided from the powers above) was that he was to drive up academic standards, a complete anathema to most practical students who creativity was their main vent and the reason they chose a BTEC course over A Level Theatre Studies.

Yes, it did have to be evidenced for qualification purposes but not to try and change it into a more academic course. Alan had fought for years to evidence students learning in more practical ways including video diaries instead of written work.

Those who started in the new academic year, of 2001 were going to have their teaching drastically altered

I felt most sorry for those second-year returners who didn't know what had hit them1

Any new leader likes to stamp their own authority in 'making it their own' but to do it as drastically and as severe made him not just unpopular with students but with some of the staff, including me!

The dedication that staff, who had devoted their lives in building the department up and would do anything for one another were not only undermined but now undervalued, so much so that the workplace, for me at least, was no fun anymore. I saw it being dismantled in front of my own eyes. Soul-destroying!

You can imagine how Brian felt in creating the course, seeing it change into the new vision of either the new Head of Department or worse, the Principalship of the college!

True, we were somewhat stuck in our ways and yes, modernisation needed to occur, but forcing out experienced staff like Brian, Jim, Angela and myself (Wendy had already retired by then and Debbie perusing a different challenge) was not the way to go about it.

Although I had joined the staff in the early nineties I knew, almost from the courses inception, just how successful we had been in providing top notch 'jobbing' performers for our very diverse industry, right up till Alan's departure, the department had helped hundreds of students achieve their ambitions and given many more the personal confidence to do, or be, whatever they wanted to in life

Glad to say those happy memories will stay with me forever whereas the latter years memories have already faded and confined to the rubbish bin. No time for negativity, I try and live my life in more positive thoughts.

It was time to move on!

52 – A NEW ROLE!

By that Christmas I couldn't preside over the dismantling of what I was so proud of in playing a small part in building up, so I ended my time in Performing Arts and transferred to the Marketing Department located at the Bispham Campus.

It obviously wasn't the same, nothing before or since, ever was!

Initially I did have fun (isn't that what life is all about?) and I will include just one anecdote from the four years spent there.

My role was a schools liaison officer going into schools selling our wares (college provision) to prospective students.

A lovely, unassuming girl named Jen helped me settle in and all went well for a while. Then a role within the department came up for grabs: a UCAS rep, travelling the country 'selling and promoting' the college at UCAS events. Prospective A-level and BTEC students who would look at the entire portfolio of courses we had to offer.

That meant I was supposed to have knowledge of all the college courses and what they entailed. Fat chance of that!

My 'acting and blagging' skills were fully deployed. Even if I say so myself, I deserved an Oscar for my performance skills not just in front of potential students at the UCAS events but, when gleaning course info from our own in-house college staff.

I'm not sure how but I actually made a difference, and enrolment through UCAS went up.

All other universities from up and down the country were represented. I even went to Ireland (which I loved) and Scotland. Obviously overnight stays were necessary for far-flung places, which gave me wonderful opportunities to explore, especially Ireland which I hadn't previously visited. Good work if you can get it!

53 – AND THAT INCLUDES YOU BOURNEMOUTH!

One particular event, a Friday as I recall, almost on home soil, at Lancaster University, my friend and neighbour from Bournemouth, expressed a desire to me, to leave early as he had a long drive back to base camp.

I agreed and said you should be able to get away early. Unfortunately, the person running the event had different ideas. He came round personally asking, if we could stay to the allotted time of 4 p.m. as some latecomers needed to be accommodated!

The guy from Bournemouth, despite this decree to stay to the bitter end, was still determined to shoot off early. His reputation had preceded him and most of the university reps knew he would be angling for an early departure. After all Bournemouth is a long way away, especially down the M6 on a Friday afternoon!

He had 'dropped me in it' previously when I had departed earlier in the week so, I owed him one.

I quietly had a word with said organiser and made him aware of 'a proposed escapee just as he was packing up. Then came a 'booming' forthright announcement over the PA.

"Can I inform all delegates that, the event finishes at 4 p.m. and therefore request all stalls to remain open till then… THAT INCLUDES YOU, BOURNEMOUTH!"

I great roar of laughter reverberated around the hall. His face was a picture as other delegates came to see him.

He knew it was me who set him up, but he had a good sense of humour, despite his delayed long journey back to the south coast!

54 – BYE BYE EVERYBODY, BYE BYE!

Although I enjoyed the travelling circus and the freedom to escape the mondain office routine it still didn't come anywhere near the rewards that Performing Art's brought.

My employers knew I was doing something right but they couldn't quite put their fingers on it, (I'm glad to say!) but, I think those who knew me better at the time did!

My little stall and 'one-man stand-up routine' went down well. I was a good salesman and recruitment numbers to our H.E provision were up. So how was I rewarded?

The powers that be decided to tie me to the office and let me train others to do my job, no thank you. As I said earlier, my form tutor at school once wrote in my report. "Putting Stephen to a desk is like trying to put a sparrow in a cage!"

They saw me as an office bound trainer, suffice to say, I most certainly did not so, I was therefore unable to 'tour' anymore!

I wasn't keen on being 'confined to barracks' Yes there were one or two nice people I worked with, (but only one or two!) Lindsay S and April H I remember but not many others!

Mainly there was a distinct shortage of fun and laughter so, after eighteen years in total, boy and (nearly) man, I left the college in 2006, never to return. (I tell a lie… I did some live links there whilst on Radio Wave).

I have been on a few college reunions from those helicon days that I look back on with such fond memories, as some of the best and happiest of my life.

The building itself was sold and is now luxury flats. There are still Pilgrimages back to the gates for photos of the front of the building, which still remains the same and appear from, time to time on the 'How Cool Was Brian Hindle' Facebook page that Lorraine H set up and still contributes to, as I'm pleased to say, so do many ex-students from all era's including some of Brian's first students who continue to post pictures and anecdotes from their times spent in that wonderful palace of dreams! Well worth a look back on to, 'rekindle the Hindle memories!

By the time I left Marketing ALL the original staff had left Performing Arts Debbie, in November 1999, shortly after our move back to Central Campus although, she did return from 2002–06.

Wendy retired not too long after the move, with Angela following sometime later. For me though the saddest departures were those of Brian and Jim.

There are very few 'practitioners' in the country of their calibre and skills. The college, if only for the students' sake, should have kept them, even if only on a part-time basis. They still had so much more to give and students, much to gain from their expertise.

There was no finer a drama teacher than Brian Hindle. Wow weren't we the lucky ones! In answering the question posed at the start, HOW COOL WAS BRIAN HINDLE? He was for me and hundreds like me, over many decades, THE COOLEST! (Credit must go to Lorraine H, for coining the How Cool phrase, although not royalties!)

It was the end of a glorious era in the Performing Arts Department that saw thousands of students start their journey, with some reaching the pinnacle of success in stage, film, TV and the music industry.

I know many aspiring Performing Arts students still take that first step with the college and as just in our time there, they too will benefit from the expertise of the current staff and the cream will still rise to the top.

Most of us who went there have benefited from the course in one form or another over the years. I know it gave me the confidence to go on and achieve more than I would have otherwise!

Brian was instrumental in that, but I also owe a debt of gratitude to all the staff who not only helped me as a student but welcomed me with open arms as a staff member.

Brian went above and beyond, not just with me but with many others to, some of which are 'house-hold names'.

In December 21 I made my annual pilgrimage to see the Panto at The Grand Theatre starring Vicky Entwistle. I caught up with her after the performance. She paid Brian a lovely tribute.

Vicky said "I owed so much to Brian, without him, none of this would have been possible"

On behalf of us all 'Thank you, Brian' for some of the happiest days of my life. You certainly deserve your accolade of 'HOW COOL WAS BRIAN HINDLE?'

Lightning Source UK Ltd.
Milton Keynes UK
UKHW021607300622
405189UK00010B/2000